THOMSON
━━━✦━━━
COURSE TECHNOLOGY
Professional ■ Technical ■ Reference

Includes

PICTURE YOURSELF
Playing Violin

Step-by-Step Instruction for Proper Fingering
and Bowing Techniques, Reading Sheet Music, and More

Bridgette Seidel

ISBN-10: 1-59863-448-8

ISBN-13: 978-1-59863-448-8

Library of Congress Catalog Card Number: 2007931840

Printed in the United States of America

08 09 10 11 12 BU 10 9 8 7 6 5 4 3 2 1

Thomson Course Technology PTR,
a division of Thomson Learning Inc.
25 Thomson Place
Boston, MA 02210
http://www.courseptr.com

Publisher and General Manager, Thomson Course Technology PTR:
Stacy L. Hiquet

Associate Director of Marketing:
Sarah O'Donnell

Manager of Editorial Services:
Heather Talbot

Marketing Manager:
Mark Hughes

Senior Editor:
Mark Garvey

Project/Copy Editor:
Kezia Endsley

Technical Reviewer:
Jennifer Day

PTR Editorial Services Coordinator:
Erin Johnson

DVD Producer:
Brandon Penticuff

Interior Layout:
Shawn Morningstar

Cover Designer:
Mike Tanamachi

Indexer:
Larry Sweazy

Proofreader:
Kate Shoup

Dedicated in loving memory to my grandmothers,
Rena Bonnie Stroud and Catalina Kennedy,
who always cherished my passion for music.

Acknowledgments

MOM AND DAD, thank you for supporting and nurturing my dreams into a real-life fairytale.

My husband, thank you for your patience, love, creative and technical input, and for the unwavering encouragement you have given to me to write this book.

Patricia, thank you for your time, effort, and careful attention to detail you put into every beautiful picture you captured to illustrate each technique throughout the book. I am proud to have such a talented and caring younger sister.

Jennifer, you are a true lifesaver, thank you for jumping in and getting the job done!

John Arnold, thank you for being the first to inspire me to play violin all those years ago, and for adding the finishing touches and transforming me into a polished violinist. I am honored to have been your student.

Charmagne, thank you for encouraging and supporting me through all of my goals in life. You are an amazing older sister.

OCU and Dean Mark Parker, thank you for believing in me and turning me into a STAR!

My students, thank you for being my inspiration.

Thank you, God, for all of the miracles in my life!

About the Author

Mrs. Bridgette Seidel graduated with a Bachelor of Music Education, Cum Laude, from Oklahoma City University. In 2000, she founded the Academy of Music Performance in Texas, and she is the Head Violin Instructor to close to 50 young violin virtuosos. Shortly after moving to Texas, she joined the performing group the BCS String Quartet as the 1st violinist, manager, and song composer. In 2004, she started a successful online business, www.videoviolinlessons.com, selling quality violin lessons on DVD. Through her easy step-by-step teaching style coupled with her adventurous and creative spirit, she has touched many hearts worldwide with the gift of music.

As a child, Bridgette was born with a weak immune system coupled with restrictive asthma, severe allergies, and had complications with ear and hearing problems that required her to have multiple ear surgeries over a number of years. Because of her poor health, Bridgette spent much of her childhood in a protective indoor environment in her home in Houston, Texas. Playing violin was one of the few things she could actively enjoy. As her love for music grew, violin quickly became her lifeboat. It was the one thing that remained a constant source of inspiration. No matter how many hospitalizations or surgeries, she could always count on the violin to fill her heart with strength and happiness. She truly believes that music and the violin helped her to overcome, persevere, and achieve a wonderful life filled with love and friendship. Above all, she is able to share her passion for the violin and music with others.

Table of Contents

Quick Start............................... 1

    Hot Cross Buns, Your First Song 2

Chapter 1   Getting Acquainted with
Your New Best Friend..................... 5

Your First Violin... 6

    The Violin Outfit... 6

    Choosing the Right Violin Size 8

Selecting a Violin... 9

    Varnish 9

    Bridge 10

    Back Side 12

    Fine Tuners 12

Selecting a Bow 13

    Before Selecting a Bow 13

    Preparing Your Bow..................................... 14

    Renting Versus Purchasing a Violin 15

Choosing Other Necessary Equipment 16

    Strings 16

    Shoulder Rest 17

    Metronome 18

    Tuner.. 18

    Metal Practice Mute 18

    Music Stand 19

Applying the Shoulder Rest and Holding the Violin............... 20

    Attaching the Shoulder Rest.............................. 20

Tuning the Strings 24

    Pizzicato Technique 24

    Tuning with the Fine Tuners and Pegs 25

Replacing Strings 26

Chapter 2   **Bowing Techniques** **29**

Pencil Hold 30
Right Hand Finger Exercises 30
Bow Placement Optimization 34
String Rolls 37
Bow Arm Movement 39
Weight Distribution of the Bow 41
        Bow Speed and Pressure 42
Bow Divisions and Rhythms 43
        Bowing Rhythms 44

Chapter 3   **Fingering Techniques** **47**

Applying Fingering Tapes 48
Setting the Hand 50
Moving the Fingers 53
        Finger Bounce 53
        Finger Strike 54
        Cross Over and Hop 54
        Elbow Swing 55
Musical ABCs 57
Finger Patterns 58
Reading Straight Across 61
Finger-Pattern Slurs 62

Chapter 4   **Music Theory** **67**

Reading Notes 68
        Note Names 68
        Violin Strings 72
        Octaves 74
        Reading Sheet Music 74
        Reading Note Names Exercises 75
Key Signatures 78
        The Order of Sharps and Flats 78
        Key Signature Names 79
        Scales 80
        Key Signature Specialties 83

Time Signatures 84

    Beats per Measure. 84

    Rhythm Exercises 85

    Rhythmic Specialties 89

Chapter 5   **Specialty Techniques. 91**

Specialty Fingerings. 92

    Ornamentation 92

    Fingering Signs. 95

    Fingering Combinations. 98

    Vibrato. 99

Specialty Bowings. 101

    Smooth Strokes 101

    Short Strokes 102

    Commanding Strokes. 104

    Bowing Sound Effects. 107

Musical Phrasing 109

    Dynamics 109

    Special Effects with Dynamics. 109

Chapter 6   **Beginner Songs. 113**

Practicing Techniques 115

Ba Ba Black Sheep 116

Lightly Row 117

Song of the Wind. 119

Go Tell Aunt Rhody 121

Ode to Joy. 123

Yellow Rose of Texas 126

On Top of Old Smoky. 129

Minuet in C 132

Minuet in G 136

Can-Can 141

She'll Be Comin' Round the Mountain. 144

The Blue Danube Waltz 147

The Mexican Hand-Clapping Song. 150

Chapter 7 **History of the Violin** **155**

Origination of the Violin 156
Famous Composers Who Were Violinists. 159
Famous Composers and Their Times 162
    The Medieval Period and the Renaissance:
    12th to 16th Centuries 162
    The Baroque Era: 17th to Mid-18th Century 162
    The Classical Era: Mid-18th to Mid-19th Century. 163
    The Romantic Era: 19th Century. 164
    The 20th Century 165

Chapter 8 **Continue the Journey** **167**

Where to Go from Here 168
Final Thoughts from Mrs. Seidel. 170

Index. **173**

Introduction

WELCOME TO THE *Picture Yourself Playing Violin* book and accompanying instructional DVD. It is both my pleasure and honor to present to you the first "how to play violin guide" of its kind. Through my many years of learning, performing, and teaching the violin, I have encountered only a handfull of instructional materials on how to play violin, yet none of these materials actually is designed to teach a true beginner how to play the violin. In general, these materials typically assume that the reader has a certain amount of prior musical knowledge, or try to fit too little information in too little time. In order to meet the needs of the true beginner wanting to learn violin, I established an on-line DVD series, which for the past three years has been transforming true beginners into wonderful violinists. Now, I have the pleasure to offer the true beginners of the world a published instruction manual that guides budding violinists through their first steps of acquiring a violin, setting up the violin to practice, actually moving the bow and fingering hands, understanding and reading sheet music, and learning how to practice a song up to a point to where you feel comfortable performing it on the violin for your first audience.

What You'll Find in This Book

The *Picture Yourself Playing Violin* book is a step-by-step guide to learning the violin. It contains a progression of easy-to-follow instructions with extremely helpful pictures and diagrams demonstrating every new technique and skill throughout the book.

This book also contains a specially produced DVD, 60 minutes in length, and jam packed with real private studio instruction covering everything from how to prepare your violin and bow, to learning the proper bowing and fingering techniques, to successfully play your first songs on the violin.

Who This Book Is For

This book is designed to transform the true beginner into a credible violinist. It is my passion to teach ordinary people how to truly understand all of the techniques and skills required to perform and master songs on the violin. I know how to break down the complexity of the violin into a progression of small and easy-to-understand steps, so that anyone can pick up a violin and play their favorite song. If you have a desire to learn how to skillfully play violin, this book is for you!

How This Book Is Organized

This book is organized in the same manner by following the same steps and methods I use in teaching true beginners taking private lessons within my own academy. I organized these steps and methods into eight technique building chapters, with each chapter covering a major aspect of the art of playing violin; for example, how to bow the violin with the right hand, finger the violin with the left hand, read sheet music, and how to learn and perform songs in an easy to follow step-by-step style of instruction. Each lesson builds on the last, which means, as you progress through the book and learn new techniques, each technique will build upon your newly learned skills.

Therefore, each lesson automatically reviews what you have previously learned while it adds a new technical aspect to your repertoire. In the book, studying each smaller lesson is similar to studying a smaller piece of a puzzle and then adding it together to understand the bigger picture, so be patient while you master each nuance of a bigger skill needed to play a major aspect of the violin. The chapters are arranged as follows:

- **Chapter 1: How to confidently select a violin and bow, hold the violin with correct posture and technique, and prepare the violin by tuning the strings.**

- **Chapter 2: How to create rich, warm, beautiful tones with the bow.**

- **Chapter 3: How to set and move each left hand finger onto the strings with accuracy and agility.**

- **Chapter 4: How to understand and read violin sheet music, note names, and rhythm like a pro.**

- **Chapter 5: How to create specialty techniques and sound effects with the left fingering hand and bow.**

- **Chapter 6: How to learn and perform 13 songs on the violin for beginners.**

- **Chapter 7: The history of the violin, with a list of famous violin makers, violinists, and how music has affected society over the centuries.**

- **Chapter 8: How to continue your music education beyond this book.**

How to Use the DVD

The accompanying DVD places the true beginner on the fast track by showing special textual elements and demonstrating the proper posture, bowing, and fingering techniques explained in the step-by-step teaching method in the book. When you learn from the DVD, it is like having a professional violin teacher in your home 24/7, ready to review or build upon and develop your skills. This DVD will cover the key topics such as how to apply your shoulder rest, tune your violin, pizzicato, bow, and finger the violin with the proper techniques, and how to create bowing and fingering sound effects. In addition, the DVD provides a performance of each beginner song with the metronome to help the student learn and perfect the art of playing violin. The student will have instant access to all of the various DVD lessons through the use of a specially designed DVD menu system that allows the viewer to quickly move from one lesson to another through the simple touch of a button.

For more violin instruction on DVD, visit www.VideoViolinLessons.com. Mrs. Seidel provides detailed note-by-note instruction with both slow and full tempo performances for each song in the Beginner, Intermediate, and Holiday DVD series.

Quick Start

Play your first song in five easy steps:

1. Hold violin: Place violin on the top of your left shoulder. Hold the violin steady with the underside of your chin and left shoulder slightly raised (see Figure QS.1).

2. Finger notes: Place your left thumb and palm line about one inch from the start of the fingerboard. When fingering, keep your wrist down and fingers round while pressing on a single string with the tips of each finger (see Figure QS.2).

3. Pizzicato notes: With your right hand, make a fist, then the letter C, and then set the thumb on the corner of the fingerboard and pull your index finger across the string like a trigger finger (see Figure QS.3).

Figure QS.1
Hold violin on your shoulder

Figure QS.2
Set fingers on the strings

Figure QS.3
Pizzicato the strings

1

4. Bow hold: Bend your thumb in the crease of the second finger and wrap your index finger over the stick. Drop your third finger, and then set the pinky round on the top of the stick. All fingers should be round, equally spaced, and leaning toward the index finger (see Figure QS.4).

5. Bow notes: Tighten the bow four turns with the screw, and rub the rosin hard on the bow hairs. Place the bow in the center between the bridge and the fingerboard. Pull the bow at a constant medium speed and medium pressure, parallel to the bridge (see Figure QS.5).

Figure QS.4
Hold the bow

Figure QS.5
Bow the strings

Hot Cross Buns, **Your First Song**

1. Pick any string.

2. Finger: 2, 1, 0 (see Figure QS.6).

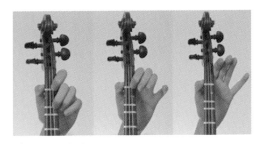

Figure QS.6
Fingering a 2, 1, 0

3. Finger: 2, 1, 0 (see Figure QS.7).

4. Finger: 2, 2, 2, 2 (see Figure QS.8).

5. Finger: 1, 1, 1, 1 (see Figure QS.9).

6. Finger: 2, 1, 0 (see Figure QS.10).

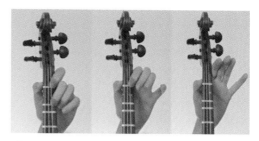

Figure QS.7
Fingering a 2, 1, 0

Work Up to Perfection

First, try to move your fingers, then pizzicato each separate finger with your right hand, and finally bow each separate note slowly.

Figure QS.8
Fingering a 2

Figure QS.9
Fingering a 1

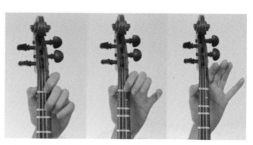

Figure QS.10
Fingering a 2, 1, 0

Getting Acquainted with Your New

Best Friend

PICTURE YOURSELF CONFIDENTLY SELECTING your first violin from a music store, knowing all of the quality names and brands that will give you the most for your money. This chapter will show you everything that a violin outfit should include and the various upgrades you can choose. You will learn the pros and cons of renting versus purchasing a violin, and how to choose the perfect size and model of violin for your age and body type. You will then build your knowledge base by learning what to look for when selecting a violin, and learning how to test a bow for quality and craftsmanship. You will be given a list of accessories for the violin that can transform any student into a true musician, and you will be shown how to use each item through easy-to-follow, step-by-step instruction. Once you have your violin, this chapter will show you how to tune all four strings using your fine tuners and pegs, how to replace strings, and how to *pizzicato* (pluck the strings with your index finger), all with perfect technique and posture.

Your First Violin

THE VIOLIN RESEMBLES THE HUMAN body, with a front side, a backside, shoulders, and a neck. At the top of the violin is the *scroll*, a decorative carving that bears a resemblance to an old fashioned scrolled piece of paper. Below the scroll is the *peg box*, which supports four pegs used to tune the four separate strings in large increments. Underneath the strings is a long black board called the *fingerboard,* which helps a violinist place finger pressure onto the strings. The four strings are supported in air by the nut at the top of the fingerboard, and the bridge in the center of the violin. The ends of the strings are connected to the *fine tuners*, used to tune the four strings in small increments. The fine tuners are attached to the *tailpiece*, and the tailpiece is attached to the violin through a black-coated wire that loops around the bottom side button. To the left and right of the bridge are the *F-holes*, which allow the sound to ring from the violin.

The Violin Outfit

Your first violin should come in a violin outfit composed of a case that stores your violin and accessories. These accessories include a sticky hardened powder called *rosin* that is rubbed on the hairs of the bow to help grip the strings of the violin, a violin with four strings and four fine tuners, and a bow.

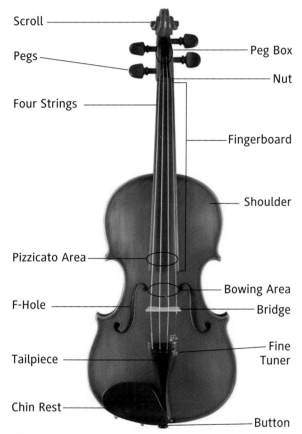

Figure 1.1
Parts of the violin

Here are the components of a violin outfit:

- *Case*—There are two main choices for violin cases. *Form fitted* is a light-weight compacted case with a hard violin-shaped shell, ideal for transporting, and *oblong* is a sophisticated upscale case with more compartments for storage.

- *Rosin*—There are two main choices for violin rosin. *Boxed rosin is* a light amber-colored rosin that comes in a wooden box, which helps protect the rosin from breaking, usually given to beginners. *Wrapped rosin* comes in light or dark colors for more specialized tone coloring and is wrapped in a soft cloth. The Hill Dark brand is perfect rosin for creating a rich, warm sound from the violin.

- *Violin*—There are two main size models for the violin. The *Stradivarius* model is a petite version of any size, perfect for smaller hands and shorter fingers, and the *Guarneri* model is the larger version of any violin size, for bigger hands and longer fingers. If you look through the left F-hole, you can see a label that identifies the model, year, and maker of a violin.

- *Bow*—There are two main material levels of bow. A *fiberglass bow* is perfect for a beginner to minimize the risk of breaking the bow accidentally. A *wooden bow*, usually made of Pernambuco or Brazilwood, gives an advanced violinist greater tone quality and more control over tone production.

Figure 1.2
Form fitted (left) and oblong (right) cases

Figure 1.4
Picture of a violin

Figure 1.3
Boxed rosin (left) and wrapped rosin (right)

Figure 1.5
Picture of a bow

Choosing the Right Violin Size

Violins come in many different sizes, ranging from toy size to full adult size, to fit the arm length of any violinist. When choosing a violin size, you want to measure your arm's length from the middle of your left palm to the side of your neck, while your left arm and hand are fully extended out perpendicular to your body. The measuring system, of extending the arm out, will translate perfectly to a correct fit. Sometimes your measurement might fall between violin sizes, in which case it is best to choose the smaller violin until your arm and hand size can fully accommodate a larger violin. The violin sizing guide in Table 1.1 provides the correspondence between your arm length and the standard violin sizes.

Figure 1.6
Measuring from palm to neck for the best fit

Table 1.1 Violin Sizing Guide

Arm Length	Approx. Age	Violin Size
14"–15.375"	4–5 years	1/16
15.375"–17"	4–5 years	1/10
17.1"–17.5"	4–5 years	1/8
17.6"–20"	5–7 years	1/4
20"–22"	7–10 years	1/2
22"–23.5"	9–11 years	3/4
23.5" and up	10 to adult	4/4 (full size)

Selecting a Violin

THIS SECTION WILL MAKE YOU into an expert when it comes to knowing what to look for when selecting a violin, by giving you the knowledge to quickly recognize the difference between low- and high-quality violins from just observing the craftsmanship. The four main components to the violin that you will need to inspect before purchasing are the varnish, bridge, backside of the violin, and fine tuners.

Varnish

The varnish, or amount of gloss on a violin, has a tremendous effect on the sound quality. The best violins have a minimal amount of varnish and staining of the wood. This allows the wood to breathe and to mature over time, which in turns gives the violin a deep, rich, warm tone in the lower notes, and a brilliant, clear, projecting tone in the upper notes. A proper amount of varnish allows you to see the grain of the wood through a natural light stain and a thin light gloss (see Figure 1.7). A violin with too much varnish has a thick painted-on color that does not show the grain of the wood and a thick overly-shiny gloss (see Figure 1.8).

Figure 1.7
A proper amount of varnish

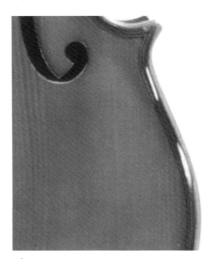

Figure 1.8
Too much varnish

Heavy Varnish

Heavy varnish creates a thick shell around the violin, which tends to dampen the sound quality and volume by closing off the pitch vibrations traveling through the wood. I also have found that the thick, shiny gloss of a violin can cause the bridge holding up the strings to lose its footing and fall off, leaving the violin unplayable.

Bridge

The bridge is held onto the violin through the downward pressure of the four strings, and is not securely attached to the front side of the violin. For this reason, the bridge can easily move out of position, affecting the volume of tone that the violin produces. The bridge also plays a critical role in the alignment of the string levels through its rounded arch shape, affecting the playability with the bow. The height of the bridge directly influences the distance between the strings to the fingerboard, affecting the playability with the left fingering hand.

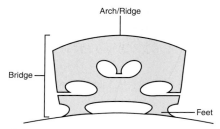

Figure 1.9
Bridge of the violin

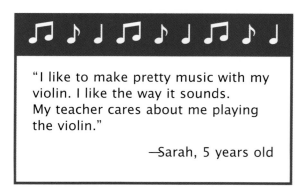

"I like to make pretty music with my violin. I like the way it sounds. My teacher cares about me playing the violin."

—Sarah, 5 years old

Here are the three ways the bridge can affect the playability of a violin:

> *Volume* is affected by the placement of the feet of the bridge, which sends the vibration frequency of a note through the front side of the violin to the *soundpost* and *bass bar* inside of the violin. The soundpost is under the left foot of the bridge and receives the vibration frequency for the higher two strings, E and A, and can easily move out of its wedged position. The bass bar is under the right foot of the bridge and receives the vibration frequency for the lower two strings, D and G, and is firmly attached to the inside of the violin. There is an exact pinpoint location on the top side of each violin in relation to the soundpost, which generates the optimal volume for every violin. For this reason, it is a good idea to have a violin craftsman give your violin a checkup every year in order to readjust the bridge and soundpost to their correct location.

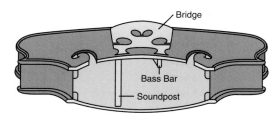

Figure 1.10
Bridge, soundpost, and bass bar

◦ The *height* of the bridge affects the energy used by the left hand to finger every note. If the bridge is too tall, the strings might be too high off the fingerboard, requiring the fingers to press down on the strings with more force than is typically needed (see Figure 1.12). The more energy used to set each finger, the quicker your hand will become exhausted. When selecting your violin, press on the strings near the F-holes at the end of the fingerboard. The strings should easily flex downward to make solid contact with the fingerboard. If the bridge is too tall, the strings will be very difficult to press down onto the fingerboard, causing your fingers to lose energy and become fatigued. If the bridge is too low, a significant amount of string will rest against the fingerboard, causing a buzzing sound when played.

◦ The *arch* of the bridge needs to be rounded, with plenty of space and height between each string. This will make playing on each separate string with the bow easier, and limits the tendency to squeak and/or hit other strings with the bow accidentally.

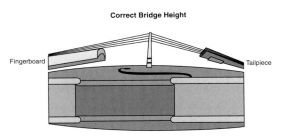

Figure 1.11
Bridge at correct height with strings to fingerboard

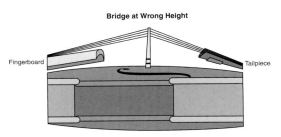

Figure 1.12
Bridge is too tall with strings to fingerboard

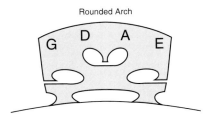

Figure 1.13
Arch of the bridge with string names

Back Side

While violin shopping, you might notice that the backs of most violins have two pieces of wood that are seamed together in the middle (see Figure 1.14), whereas other violins have a back side made out of a single piece of wood (see Figure 1.15). This does not play a great role in the quality or price of a violin, but there is a technical difference between the two variations. A one-piece back tends to be stronger, giving more support to the underside of the violin, causing the violin to be louder. A two-piece back, on the other hand, might become unglued and split open over time.

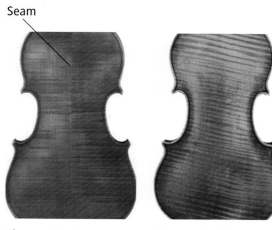

Seam

Figure 1.14
Back side of the violin, two pieces

Figure 1.15
Back side of the violin, one piece

Fine Tuners

A fine tuner allows a string to be easily tuned by stretching or loosening the string in tiny increments. You might notice that some violins have four fine tuners, one for each string, and others have only an E string fine tuner on the far right side of the tail piece. Having four fine tuners makes it easier to tune a violin without the threat of accidentally breaking a string from using the pegs, making it ideal for beginners (see Figure 1.16). The pegs tune the strings in large increments, and in the hands of an unskilled violinist, can stretch a string past its appropriate pitch to the string's breaking point (see Figure 1.17). Advanced players are skilled in using the pegs to tune all of the string, and only use a fine tuner for the delicate E string. If you are a true beginner, you should purchase a violin will all four fine tuners or have a music store add the fine tuners to your violin.

Figure 1.16
The four fine tuners

G D A E

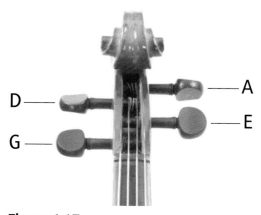

D

G

A

E

Figure 1.17
The four pegs

Selecting a Bow

THE BOW IS THE SINGING VOICE of the violin. This section will help you judge the difference between low- and high-quality bows by giving you the knowledge of how to properly test a bow for superior craftsmanship.

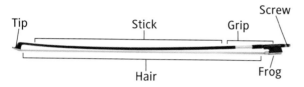

Figure 1.18
Parts of the bow

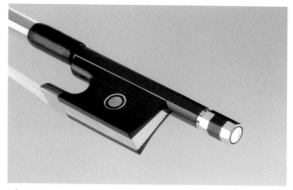

Figure 1.19
Octagonal shaped bow

Before Selecting a Bow

The shape of a bow is a personal choice. I prefer a light thin bow for greater control over tiny musical expressions. A thicker bow gives more weight for a louder volume, but tends to be stiff, making it difficult to control and achieve soft musical expressions. I also prefer an octagonal shaping on the wood verses round shaping on the wood. The octagonal shaping has a gradual increase and decrease in weight throughout the entire length of the bow, which evenly distributes the vibrations traveling through the wood of the bow.

There is an easy way to check the bow for any signs of warping or sideways curving of the wood. First, tighten the bow a pinky's width in the middle, by turning the screw at the end of the bow clockwise to the right (see Figure 1.21). Hold the bow vertically, and rotate the stick of the bow toward you until you see the white of the hair equally lining the left and right sides of the wood (see Figure 1.20). If the bow is straight, the hair should line the wood equally from tip to frog. If the bow were warped, you would see the wood curve away from the hair, bending sideways to the left or to the right side, usually in the middle of the bow. A warped bow gives an unpredictable bounce and makes it hard to control the tone quality, whereas a straight bow gives greater control of tone and texture for each note.

Figure 1.20
Warp check, holding the bow vertical

Preparing Your Bow

The bow and rosin work together to grip the string, generating a solid tone from the violin. First, you must tighten the bow to a pinky's width in the middle by turning the screw at the end of the bow clockwise to the right (see Figure 1.21). After the bow has been tightened, you can apply the rosin, by rubbing the sticky powder that forms on the top of the rosin onto the hair of the bow (see DVD). If your rosin is new, you might want to start the powder by lightly scratching the top of the rosin. Once the rosin powder is started, rub the rosin against the hair in four or five smooth long strokes covering the entire length of the bow hair with hard pressure. A violinist needs to rosin the bow hair only once or twice per week. Remember to loosen your bow hair every time you place it back in the case.

Figure 1.21
Tightening the bow a pinky's width in the middle

Renting Versus Purchasing a Violin

Renting a violin is generally a good idea for young players. Renting allows a young violinist to upgrade the size and quality of his or her violin as the violinist grows physically, and matures in technical skills on the violin. Be sure the dealer you are working with has a short-term return policy and a long-term trade or purchase policy that will allow you to accrue rental credit toward the purchase of a violin. Rental violins, in general, are lower quality and have been used by multiple beginner students who might have abused the violin. When selecting a rental violin, take into consideration the age of the violin as physical damage accumulates over time. You may also ask for a new set of Thomastik Dominant strings to be placed on the violin.

Purchasing a violin has multiple advantages for the serious violinist. When you purchase a violin, you can select your starting price and quality. Over time, you can also trade the violin in for upgrades in terms of size and price. Purchasing a violin secures a new violin or a violin that has been previously played upon by a serious, advanced violinist. A new violin requires daily practice over a long period of time to mature and open the tone quality of the violin, whereas the tone quality of an older violin that has been performed on by advanced violinist should be already fully opened to a rich, warm, deep tone.

The wood of the violin is almost a living organism because it matures, breathes, and constantly learns from its owner. A beginner can degrade a violin by teaching it to sing only bad tones. On the other hand, a violin can increase its worth by learning to sing beautiful tones from an advanced player. A new violin guarantees a perfectly adjusted violin, but you will need to practice daily, focusing on tone-developing techniques. A previously used violin has a developed tone, but because the previous player will have influenced that tone, you should be aware of the previous owner's skill level.

"Violin is a great instrument to play, because to play the violin correctly, you need lots of concentration. The violin has taught me how to concentrate to achieve my goals, even on non-musical challenges."

—Ruby, 10 years old

Choosing Other Necessary Equipment

OVER THE YEARS OF TEACHING violin, I have discovered certain brands and equipment that have stood the test of time in terms of their durability, price, and effectiveness to help simplify the intimidating task of learning violin. In today's market, these accessories are in the low end of cost and the high end of reliability and quality. In this section I will identify some of the best strings, shoulder rests, metronomes, tuners, and stands that will give you the most bang for your buck.

Strings

The right strings can make a big difference on how a violin sounds. The Thomastik Dominant brand of strings are the best strings for a beginner or intermediate player, because they give a clean-clear tone, rich in overtones (see Figure 1.22). In addition, these strings tend to last a full six months in any climate conditions as they are impervious to changes in humidity, allowing for stable intonation and a long life. For a long-lasting professional string, I prefer the Pirastro brand with the Evah Pirazzi strings for a bright brilliant tone (see Figure 1.23), and the Obligato strings for a darker warm tone (see Figure 1.24). Both strings have a wide dynamic range, intense with brilliant colorations, and quick response to both fingers and bow articulation. The tone differences between the brands are created by different materials and the thickness of the gauge used to make each string. When selecting a set of strings, you must request strings according to the size of your violin and decide between a loop or ball E string, depending on the style of your fine tuner. If your fine tuner is shaped

like a hook, you will need a loop E string. If your fine tuner is shaped with a split down the center, then you will need a ball E string. The A, D, and G strings always have ball ends attached.

Figure 1.22
Dominant strings

Figure 1.23
Evah Pirazzi strings

Figure 1.24
Obligato strings

Selecting Strings

When given the option to choose the gauge and material of your strings, choose a medium gauge on all four strings and a gold E string for bright and clear-sounding tones.

Shoulder Rest

A shoulder rest can make holding the violin much easier by allowing the violinist to grip the violin comfortably between the underside of the chin and the top of the shoulder. My favorite full-size shoulder rest is the Wolf "Forte" Primo because it can extend to any height and has a non-slip grip (see Figure 1.25). A Kun original is great for all the various violin sizes; they are fully adjustable in size and height, and extremely durable (see Figure 1.26). A small child might prefer to use a dry, natural sponge held onto the violin by rubber bands, because sponges are super flexible and easy to use (see Figure 1.27). You can also cut away some of the thickness of the sponge for a custom fit.

Figure 1.26
Kun original

Figure 1.25
Wolf "Forte" Primo

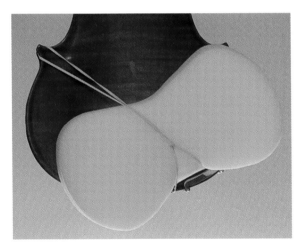

Figure 1.27
Violin with a sponge attached

Metronome

A *metronome* is an accessory for the violin that can transform a student into a true musician. A metronome provides a steady counting beat at any tempo, guiding and reassuring the musician for all rhythmic variations. The Wittner Taktell Piccolo gives a loud "tick tock" and requires no batteries (see Figure 1.28). For a classic upscale version of this metronome, try a Wittner Traditional Pyramid Metronome with its mahogany hardwood finish (see Figure 1.29). Both of the Wittner metronomes keep a steady beat by a moving pendulum. The beat can be changed to any desired tempo by adjusting the sliding weight attached to the shaft of the pendulum.

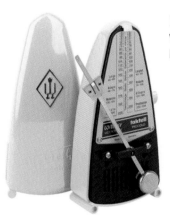

Figure 1.28
Wittner Taktell
Piccolo metronome

Figure 1.29
Wittner Traditional
Pyramid metronome

Tuner

Violin strings needs to be tuned every day, and a good tuner is a violinist's best friend. I have found that the Seiko SAT500 Auto-Chromatic Tuner is the easiest to use. Just press the Power button, then play any string, and it will tell you automatically what note you are playing and how far you are from the correct pitch. You do not need to push any other buttons to tune different pitches.

Figure 1.30
Seiko SAT500 auto-chromatic tuner

Metal Practice Mute

A *metal practice mute* is the perfect accessory for the violin for when you want to practice the violin without disturbing anyone around you. The generic metal practice mute works by fitting snuggly onto the top of the bridge and over the four strings; this minimizes the amount of vibrations from the string to the bridge, significantly reducing the loudest of notes to a soft whisper.

Figure 1.31
Metal practice mute

Music Stand

The ideal music stand should be able to hold your music at any height. I prefer the Hamilton two-section music stand for easy transporting; it folds up, can be easily stowed in a carrying bag, and features music clips to hold sheet music in place (see Figure 1.32). The Manhasset Tall Symphony music stand is the ultimate practice stand. It is ideal for standing musicians and others who need extra height, for it extends to a maximum height of 60 inches from floor to shelf, and it can be used with stand extenders that will display multiple pages of sheet music at the same time (see Figure 1.33).

Here's the proper way to set up your folding two-section music stand:

1. Fold down the tripod legs into the locking position.

2. Release the clamp on the top of the shaft to raise the center pipe.

3. Push down the clamp on the top of the shaft to secure the height.

4. Insert the top end of the pipe into the backside of the music holder.

5. Spread open the music holder until the bottom shelf is flat.

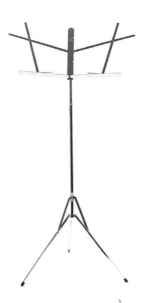

Figure 1.32
Hamilton two-section music stand

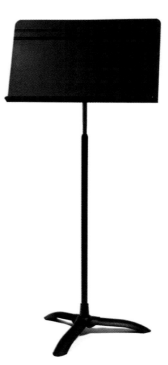

Figure 1.33
Manhasset Tall Symphony music stand

Applying the Shoulder Rest and Holding the Violin

YOUR BODY LANGUAGE, and the way you hold your instrument, speaks volumes when it comes to your skill level. Picture two violinists performing. One violinist slouches his head down with his violin pointing to the floor, and the other violinist stands tall with his shoulders back and his violin held high. Which one do you think is a better violinist?

Attaching the Shoulder Rest

Here's how to attach a shoulder rest to your violin (see DVD):

1. While sitting, place the violin on your lap with the front of the violin facing you, and place the scroll of the violin on your left shoulder so that your body holds the leaning violin securely.

2. Grip the legs of the shoulder rest between your first two fingers of each hand, with the bar of the shoulder rest away from you and the thicker side, or the side that dips downward, near your left hand.

3. Place two feet on the left back side of the violin near the top of the violin curve, and then place the other two feet on the right back side, near the bottom button of the violin.

4. With your right hand, wiggle up the two feet along the rim of the violin with your right hand until the shoulder rest feels securely attached, near the bottom of the violin. Refer to Figure 1.25 to attach a Wolf, Figure 1.26 to attach a Kun, and Figure 1.27 to attach a sponge.

Figure 1.34
Attaching the shoulder rest

Figure 1.35
The attached shoulder rest

Kun Length

If Your Kun is too small or too long for your violin, you can change the length by adjusting the screws on the underside of the bar.

Applying a Sponge

Link two rubber bands together. Place one loop around the chin rest and stretch the length of the joined rubber bands under the violin, across and over the sponge, until the other loop of the joined rubber bands can hook around the back-lower corner of the right side of the violin.

Here's how to place the violin into proper playing position (see DVD):

1. Rest position is when you hold your violin on your right hip with your right hand holding the bottom side of the violin and your left hand holding the bottom shoulder of the violin (see Figure 1.36).

Figure 1.36
Rest position

2. To take the violin into playing position, hold the shoulder of the violin with your left hand, extend your left arm, and flip the violin upside down, counterclockwise (see Figure 1.37). Place your right index finger onto the bottom button.

Figure 1.37
Turning the violin upside down

3. Bring the violin over your left shoulder until the index finger of your right hand, on the bottom button of the violin, touches the center of your neck. See Figure 1.38.

Figure 1.38
The violin in playing position

4. Gently secure the violin with the underside of your chin in the chin rest and your left shoulder slightly raised.

5. Slowly release your hands from the violin and place your arms down by your sides, holding the violin parallel to the floor with only your chin and shoulder. Be very careful not to drop the violin. At this point, you should be standing comfortably with the violin balanced between the underside of your chin and the top of your shoulder, as shown in Figure 1.39.

Figure 1.39
Arms down while the violin is in playing position

6. Turn your body toward the right side of the music stand, so that the scroll of the violin is pointing toward the center of the stand. Your feet should be separated, with your left foot pointing to the stand, balancing your weight equally on both feet.

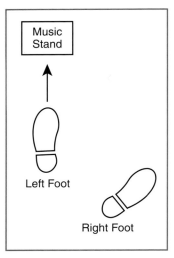

Figure 1.40
Violin stance

Sitting Position

If you would like to sit while practicing the violin, sit on the right corner of the chair near the front edge. Keep your back straight, and place equal weight on both of your legs and feet. Do not lean against the back of the chair.

Figure 1.41
Body posture while sitting

Here's how to adjust your shoulder rest for a perfect fit:

1. Hold the violin in playing position, without the shoulder rest.

2. With your shoulders relaxed and your head held high, lift the violin so that the chin rest touches the underside of your chin.

3. Use your right hand to measure the distance from the top of your shoulder to the violin, and then from the bottom of your collar bone to the violin.

4. Adjust the screw's height on the shoulder rest to fit the natural gap between you and the violin.

Figure 1.42
Measuring the distance to adjust the shoulder rest

How the Shoulder Rest Lays on Your Shoulder

The thick end of the shoulder rest, or the end that bends toward the violin, should lie on the top middle of your shoulder, between your arm and your neck. The skinny end, or end that curves away from the violin, should rest near the bottom part of your collar bone. See Figure 1.43.

Figure 1.43
Shoulder rest, placed properly on the shoulder

Tuning the Strings

TUNING THE VIOLIN IS A SIMPLE process if you have four fine tuners and Seiko SAT500 auto-chromatic tuner. Press the Power button on your tuner and, without touching any other buttons, it should automatically read 440 Hz and in the key of C. Once you have the tuner ready, you need to listen to the pitch of a violin string by pizzicato, or plucking the string.

Pizzicato Technique

Pizzicato is the art of playing violin by plucking a string with your right index finger to create a short, ringing, percussive tone. All beginners learn how to play the violin through pizzicato because it requires no background experience and little technique to form a good sounding tone from the violin.

Here's the proper way to pizzicato a note (see the DVD):

1. Place the violin in playing position and make a fist with the right hand.

2. Create the letter "C" with your thumb and index finger (see Figure 1.44).

3. Place the thumb on the corner of the finger-board.

4. Set the side of your hand on top of the violin wood.

5. Move your index finger like a trigger finger.

Figure 1.44
Right hand, fist, letter "C"

6. Grip a string with the pad of your index finger and pull over the string with medium force, creating a plucking sound. When plucking any of the four strings, you want to keep your index finger around two inches from the end of the fingerboard (see Figure 1.45).

Figure 1.45
Index finger gripping the A string

Tuning with the Fine Tuners and Pegs

Each pitch can be adjusted three ways: flat ♭, natural ♮, and sharp ♯ (see Figure 1.46). When musicians talk about notes, they must be specific in naming a note with its sign, like A♭ and A♯. Every note is natural unless stated otherwise by a flat or a sharp sign, so it is common to see a note without a symbol in music, which means you should play that note a natural.

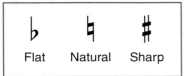

Figure 1.46
Flat, natural, and sharp

Flat   Natural   Sharp

Pitch Levels on the Tuner

When tuning the violin strings with an auto-chromatic tuner, be sure to tune the G string to a G3 pitch level, the D string to a D4 pitch level, the A string to an A4 pitch level, and the E string to an E5 pitch level.

Using the auto-chromatic tuner and the pizzicato technique, pluck the E string, and notice the pitch note on the screen. If it reads E or E♮, but the needle is pointing to the flat ♭ or to the sharp ♯, use your fine tuner to correct the pitch.

Place your violin in playing position, and bring your left hand under the violin and up to the right side of your neck. Angle your hand so that you can grip the fine tuners between your thumb and index finger (see Figure 1.47). If your tuner shows the pitch is flat, roll your left index finger up to raise the pitch up. If the tuner shows the pitch is sharp, roll your left index finger down to move the

pitch down. If the tuner reads an E♭ or D♭, or a note lower than E♮, you must raise the pitch quite a bit. If the tuner reads an E♯ or an F♮, or a note higher than E♮, you must lower the note quite a bit (see Figure 1.48). (see the DVD)

Figure 1.47
Body posture to tune with the fine tuners

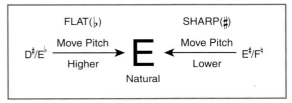

Figure 1.48
Directional chart showing a flat, natural, sharp pitch

To move the pitch great distances, find the matching peg to the "out-of-tune" string and slowly rotate the peg away from you to raise the pitch or toward you to lower it (see Figure 1.49). To keep the peg from slipping, as you turn the peg, push it firmly into the wood of the peg box, to seat it securely. (see the DVD)

Figure 1.49
Body posture to tune with the pegs

Replacing Strings

A VIOLINIST NEEDS TO REPLACE all four strings every six months to ensure optimal tone quality and pitch accuracy. When replacing all four strings, it is important to alternate strings, removing and replacing one string at a time before moving to the next string, so that there are always at least three strings to hold the bridge in place. I like to start with the A string and then the G and E strings, and lastly the D string.

Here's how to replace a string:

1. Set the violin in your lap, strings facing you. Remove the old string by turning the matching peg down toward you, loosening the string and enabling you to pull the string off the violin (refer to Figure 1.49).

2. Thread the new string through the peg hole until you see the yarn-wrapped end of the string sticking out through the other side of the peg (see Figure 1.50).

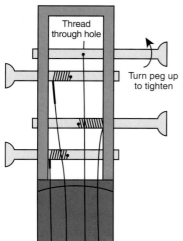

Figure 1.50
Threading the string through the peg hole

Thread through hole

Turn peg up to tighten

3. Turn the peg up, wrapping the string around the peg in an orderly fashion toward the side of the peg box. Make sure you do not cross the string over itself as you are winding it toward the peg box (see Figure 1.51).

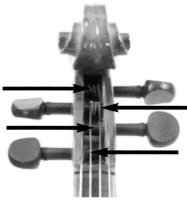

Figure 1.51
Wrapping the string toward the peg box

4. After a few turns, attach the ball at the other end of the string to the matching fine tuner or insert the ball inside the matching hole in the tail piece.

5. Keep tightening the string as you make sure it is lined up in the nut and in the bridge groove. Keep plucking the string while you turn the peg and use the auto-chromatic tuner until you have reached the desired pitch.

6. Once you have replaced all four strings, you will need to check the bridge to make sure it's not tilting or leaning toward the fingerboard of the violin (see Figure 1.52). If the bridge seems to be leaning, carefully grip the top of the bridge with your two thumbs and gently nudge it back to an upright position (see Figure 1.53).

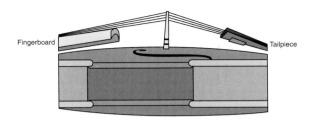

Figure 1.54
Upright bridge

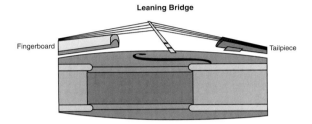

Figure 1.52
Leaning bridge

Settling a String

The strings will need to be tuned repeatedly (10 to 15 times) until the strings stretch and settle, and hold their natural pitch.

Figure 1.53
Adjusting the bridge with thumbs

"I like discovering new musical notes on my violin, and playing my favorite songs with the bow."

—Colin, 10 years old

Bowing
Techniques

PICTURE YOURSELF IN THE MOMENT prior to
performing a heart-felt solo on the violin. Your violin is
positioned with confidence, you have an elegant bow
hand holding the bow just above that perfect singing spot on
the string, and you begin your first gorgeous note as you exhale
and relax into the sounds of the violin swirling around you.
This chapter is designed to teach you how to elegantly hold
your bow, find that perfect singing spot on the violin, and
move your bow arm with ease, while creating different-sounding
textures and rhythms.

Pencil Hold

THE FIRST STEP IN LEARNING to use the bow is to learn how to position each finger properly on the grip of the bow with the correct spacing. I prefer using an ordinary, unsharpened pencil with a hexagon shape, because a pencil has nearly the same shape as the bow grip. The pencil is lightweight, so you will not over strain your fingers, and you can take a pencil anywhere to practice at any time, which makes learning the bow hold on a pencil ideal.

Here's how to learn the violin bow hold by practicing with a pencil (see the DVD):

1. Make sure all your fingernails are shortly trimmed. With your right hand, place the tip of your thumbnail into the first crease from the end of your second finger, and form a circle in the center of the attached fingers (see Figure 2.1).

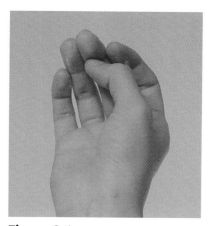

Figure 2.1
Thumbnail in crease of the second finger

2. Insert the middle of the pencil between your thumb tip and the crease of your second finger (see Figure 2.2).

Figure 2.2
Pencil between thumb tip and second finger

3. Lean your hand to the left, so that the pencil rests securely in the space between the first and second knuckles, and touch the pad of your index finger along the side of the pencil (see Figure 2.3).

Figure 2.3
Leaning to the index finger

4. Drop your third finger comfortably.

5. Set a round pinky on the top of the pencil (see Figure 2.4).

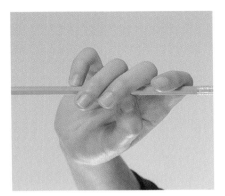

Figure 2.4
Drop your third finger and round the pinky on top

Finger Spacing

There should be equal space between the knuckles of each finger, and make sure that the thumb is bent with a freshly trimmed thumbnail pushing into the wood of the pencil.

"My advice for violinists of all ages is to persevere. Do not give up, even when you can't seem to get it right. Just start from the beginning and try it again. I bet that eventually you can get it correct if you keep trying."

—Ankur, 11 years old.

Right Hand Finger Exercises

THE VIOLIN BOW HOLD NEEDS TO BE flexible, absorbing the tiniest of vibrations from the bow like little bendable springs. There are two exercises to get your fingers moving, called "Claw Up and Straight Down" and "Claw Side to Side Extensions." These exercises are designed to help your fingers and wrist learn the proper movement and flexibility needed to cushion the transition between each bow stroke when playing the violin.

Here's how to practice the first finger exercise, "Claw Up and Straight Down" (see the DVD):

1. Hold your right hand chest high and, with the palm facing downward, extend your fingers straight out (see Figure 2.5).

Figure 2.5
Hand up, palm down

2. Without moving the arm or hand, form a claw with your fingers, rounding and bending the finger knuckles higher than the hand knuckles (see Figure 2.6).

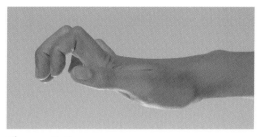

Figure 2.6
Claw hand

3. Without moving the arm or hand, drop and straighten your fingers straight down (see Figure 2.7).

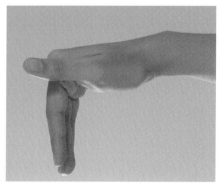

Figure 2.7
Fingers are straight down

4. Repeat steps 2–3 until your fingers are fully flexible.

Here's how to practice the second fingering exercise, called "Claw Side to Side Extensions" (see the DVD):

1. Hold your right hand chest high and, with the palm facing downward, set your fingers in the claw position.

2. Without moving the arm or hand, bend your wrist to the right and extend your fingers out to the right, so they are flat with your hand and angled to the extreme far right (see Figure 2.8).

Figure 2.8
Fingers angled right

3. Return your fingers back to the claw position with a straight wrist (see Figure 2.9).

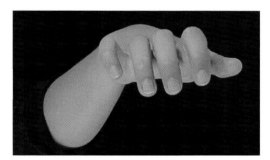

Figure 2.9
Fingers in claw position

4. Without moving the arm or hand, bend your wrist to the left and extend your fingers out to the left, so they are flat with your hand and angled to the extreme far left (see Figure 2.10).

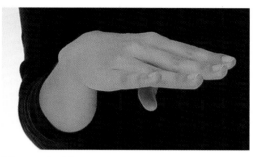

Figure 2.10
Fingers angled left

5. Repeat steps 2–4 until your fingers can fully extend from side to side.

How to Practice Both Exercises (see the DVD)

Both exercises should be practiced three ways: with unattached fingers; with the thumb bent in the crease of the second finger; and with the proper bow hold on the pencil. When you practice both exercises with the pencil, try to keep the same finger placement on the pencil while bending and straightening the knuckles. Be very careful not to adjust the fingers or roll the pencil between the fingers while you try to achieve your full range of motion.

Bow Placement Optimization

OPTIMIZATION OF BOW PLACEMENT is used to determine the exact location on the string and the angle of the bow to the string that gives you the best tone quality on every note. If learned properly, this exercise will eliminate squeaks and provide you with a rich warm tone. The optimal location to place your bow on the string is in the middle between your bridge and fingerboard, with the bow parallel to the bridge and at a right angle with the string. If the bow is set diagonally to the strings or to the bridge, it will produce an undesirable unfocused tone from the bow hair's not gripping the string properly.

> "When I started playing violin, I never thought I would be able to perform by myself, but with the help of Mrs. Seidel I have been able to play in front of crowds and I am able to play much better. I have gone from being last chair of the 2nd violin section to a much better chair as a 1st violinist. With Mrs. Seidel's teaching skills, I have improved so much."
>
> —Sarah, 13 years old

Here's how to place your bow hold onto the bow (see the DVD):

1. With your bow rosined and tightened a pinky's width in the middle, use your left hand to hold the bow chest high by gripping the stick and pointing the frog to the right. Now your right hand can freely practice applying the same pencil hold onto the grip of the bow.

2. Place your right thumb at the end of the black cushy grip, near the hump of the frog. Angle your arm so that the thumb is pointing straight up, pushing the shortened thumb nail against the wood of the bow and letting the bottom part of your bent thumb touch the hairs of the bow (see Figure 2.11).

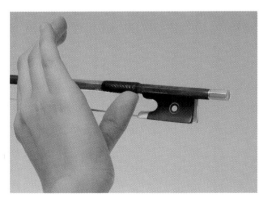

Figure 2.11
Bow thumb placement

3. Set the crease of the second finger on the stick, directly above the thumb (see Figure 2.12).

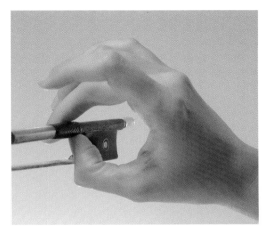

Figure 2.12
Second finger above the thumb

4. Lean your hand to the index finger, placing the stick between the first and second knuckles (see Figure 2.13).

Figure 2.13
Index finger on the bow

5. Drop your third finger comfortably over the frog of the bow.

6. Set a round pinky on top of the stick, near your third finger (see Figure 2.14).

Figure 2.14
Third finger and pinky on bow

Here's how to locate the bow placement optimization on your strings (see the DVD):

1. Stand in front of a large mirror and place your violin in playing position.

2. If you need to set your bow hold onto your bow, cross your left hand under the violin and hold the bow in the lower half, and carefully apply your bow hold (see Figure 2.15).

Figure 2.15
Left hand holding the bow in playing position

3. Set your left hand on the right shoulder of the violin to hold the violin steady.

4. Place the middle of the bow on the A string in the center of the string between the bridge and the fingerboard (see Figure 2.16).

Figure 2.16
Bow centered on the A string

5. Position your body so that your right side is turned toward the mirror at a 45-degree angle.

6. Use the mirror to straighten your bow so that it is parallel to the bridge and at a right angle to the strings (see Figure 2.17).

Figure 2.17
Straight bow on the A string

7. Repeat steps 4–6 to find the bow placement optimization for the tip, middle, and frog of the bow. Be sure not to pull the bow across the strings to get to different sections of the bow; instead just lift and set the bow on each string near the tip, middle, and frog of the bow. While practicing this exercise, notice the different positions your wrist and arm assume when keeping the bow properly aligned with the bridge and strings at each new section of the bow.

Remember to Check Technique

Every few moments, do a bow hold check as follows: "thumb bent, pinky round, and shoulders down and relaxed."

String Rolls

IN THIS SECTION, YOU WILL LEARN to roll the bow to different strings by raising and lowering the arm through the arm socket of the right shoulder, and at the same time you will learn the height position of your arm for each string level This rolling action will also show you how much "wiggle room" is between each string level so that you can learn to play on a single string, preventing a squeaking tone from occurring by accidentally leaning against other surrounding strings.

> "Bach once said, 'There's nothing remarkable about it. All one has to do is hit the right keys at the right time and the instrument plays itself.' Good luck to you as you begin your musical journey."
>
> —Chen, 15 years old

Here's how to practice string rolls (see the DVD):

1. Place the violin in playing position with a proper bow hold onto the bow. To help hold the violin steady, you can set your left hand onto the right shoulder of the violin.

2. Using a large mirror, place a straight bow (parallel to the bridge) in the middle of the bow, on the E string.

3. Keep the elbow at a right angle with the arm, as if the arm is in a cast, and keep the shoulder down and relaxed (see Figure 2.18).

Figure 2.18
String rolls, arm at right angle

4. Slowly raise and lower the entire arm through the arm socket to roll the bow over all four strings. Be careful not to make a sound by accidentally pulling the bow across the strings (see Figure 2.19).

Figure 2.19
String rolls, on G string

5. Notice your arm level for each string, and experiment with rolling to different combinations of strings while calling out the string names.

6. Repeat steps 3–5 while experimenting with the string rolls near the tip, middle, and frog of the bow. Notice the different positions your wrist and arm assume while keeping the bow properly aligned with the bridge and strings at each new section of the bow.

Roll the Bow

Most beginners have trouble bowing on a single string, instead always squeaking and leaning on the surrounding strings. A quick fix to determine how much wiggle room you have between each string is to string roll on a single string as far as you can without touching the surrounding strings. Try this at the tip, middle, and frog of the bow on each string.

"I selected the violin because I thought it would be fun to learn a string instrument and compete against my brother, who plays the viola. I like the violin because I can bring out a great sound to please myself and other people."

—Kelly, 11 years old

Bow Arm Movement

THE MOVEMENT OF THE BOW ARM is designed to draw the bow straight (parallel to the bridge) from the frog down to the tip of the bow and back up to the frog of the bow, to create a full rich warm tone. This movement can be categorized in four arm positions: cross over, cross back, open elbow, and close elbow. To learn each of the four bow arm positions, and how to transition seamlessly between each position, practice with your bow hold on a pencil by *air bowing*.

Here's how to practice the four bow arm positions with the pencil (see the DVD):

- *Cross over*—With the pencil in your bow hold, bend your wrist upward, angled to your nose. Your shoulder should be relaxed while your arm/elbow hangs downward, crossed over your chest (see Figure 2.20).

- *Cross back*—Keep the elbow closed and move your upper arm down to the side of your rib cage while you flatten your wrist (see Figure 2.21).

Figure 2.21
The cross-back arm position

Figure 2.20
The cross-over arm position

- *Open elbow*—Open the elbow until your arm is straight and flip your wrist downward (see Figure 2.22).

Figure 2.22
The open-elbow arm position

- *Close elbow*—Close and drop your elbow slightly to form a right angle with your arm and a flat wrist (see Figure 2.23).

Figure 2.23
The close-elbow arm position

Repeat the four bow arm positions until you feel comfortable blending all four steps into one smooth motion.

Invisible Track

Keep your pencil straight as you practice the four bow arm positions. Imagine that the pencil is moving along an invisible track that extends the full length of your bow arm (see Figure 2.24).

Bowing
Track

Figure 2.24
Invisible track

Weight Distribution of the Bow

WHEN YOU DIVIDE THE WEIGHT of the bow in its three main parts—tip, middle, and frog—you will find that each section of the bow weighs differently according to the thickness of the wood and the mechanics attached to the bow (see Figure 2.25 and the DVD). If a violinist desires a constant volume of tone from the frog to the tip of the bow, the violinist will need to equalize the bow's natural weight distribution as it is pulled against the string by simply adjusting the arm weight and finger pressure on the bow hold.

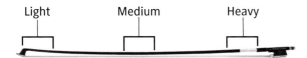

Figure 2.25
Weight sections of the bow

- The frog has the most weight, with the thickest part of the wood, the mechanics of the frog, and the hand/arm weight resting on the string.

- The middle of the bow is the neutral section, with a medium weight resting on the string.

- The tip of the bow is very light, with only the thinnest part of the wood resting on the string.

This unequal weight distribution forces the violinist to have various bow pressures to equalize the weight of the bow when moving the bow across the string from frog to tip, and from tip to frog of the bow.

Here's how to equalize the weight of the bow to create a constant and steady tone volume (see the DVD):

1. Place the violin in playing position with a proper bow hold on the bow, and set a straight bow on the A string near the frog. To help hold the violin steady, you can set your left hand on the right shoulder of the violin.

2. As you start "down" bow, move the bow down toward the floor and away from the frog with a quick starting speed and minimal pressure onto the string by balancing the bow's weight off the string with your round pinky.

3. When the bow approaches the middle, the pressure normalizes to a medium pressure and the weight is balanced between the middle two fingers of your bow hold.

4. As you near the tip, you must apply more pressure by leaning into the bow with your thumb and index finger of your right hand.

5. Reverse the process as you change direction to "up" bow (or up to the ceiling) by transferring the pressure from the index finger through the middle two fingers of your hand until you reach the frog of the bow, where you balance the weight of the bow with the round pinky of your bow hold.

Bowing Direction

Down bow is when you move from the frog to the tip of the bow. *Up bow* is when you move from the tip to the frog of the bow. To remember the bowing direction, think: Move the bow down to the floor, and up to the ceiling.

Bouncing Bow

Every bow has a *sweet spot,* usually in the middle where the bow likes to bounce or skip. This bounce is very useful in certain advanced specialty bowings, but sometimes frustrating when you want to make a long smooth tone. If your bow bounces uncontrollably, try loosening the tension of your bow hair and pinpoint the sweet spot. Once identified, apply greater controlled pressure when crossing over that section in the bow.

Bow Speed and Pressure

Bow speed and pressure is just as critical to a violinist as air flow is to a singer. The bow speed and pressure creates the voice of the violin. Sometimes the violin can sing beautiful tones, and sometimes the violin can sing bad tones. In order to play beautiful tones on a violin, the violinist needs to prevent bad tones. In order to prevent bad tones from occurring, a violinist must first feel the speed and pressure of the bow against the string that can create a bad tone. There are three categories of bad tone: crunchy, glazy, and pressed.

Here's how to create the three categories of bad tones (see the DVD):

- *Crunchy tone*—Moving the bow too slowly at the frog with too much pressure allows the bow hairs to grip the string too much.

- *Glazy tone*—Moving the bow too quickly at the tip with little pressure doesn't allow the bow to grip the string, creating an unfocused pitch.

- *Pressed tone*—Moving the bow at a medium speed while subtly increasing the pressure on the string in the middle of the bow forces the pitch of the string to bend downward, on the brink of a crunchy tone.

Once you have discovered how to create all three of the bad tones, try to alternate your bow strokes from bad tones to good tones. Notice the subtle change in bow speed or pressure that can change a good tone into a bad tone, and a bad tone back into a good tone.

Speed and Pressure

A good rule of thumb is to move the bow at a medium speed and medium pressure for good tone quality.

Bow Divisions and Rhythms

A VIOLINIST USES DIFFERENT PARTS of the bow to generate various sound effects and rhythms. This section will give you the fundamental skills to use your bow to discover the different ways tone can be affected by certain combinations of bow placement, speed, and pressure.

The bow has three main divisions (see Figure 2.26):

- Upper half (UH) allows the bow arm to move freely and quickly near the tip of the bow.

- Lower half (LH) requires the bow arm to move with greater precision and control near the frog of the bow.

- Whole bow (WB) uses the bow arm's full range of motion, covering the entire length of the bow.

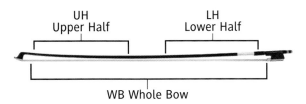

Figure 2.26
Divisions of the bow

These divisions can be generalized into three main sections (see Figure 2.27):

- The frog (F) of the bow produces louder and more forceful tones.

- The middle (M) of the bow produces a normal blend of tones.

- The tip (T) of the bow produces smoother and more delicate tones.

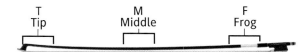

Figure 2.27
Sections of the bow

"I selected the violin because it is fun to play, and the music that it creates makes me feel good inside. I feel very special because I know how to play an instrument like the violin."

—Wenwen, 9 years old

Bowing Rhythms

Now that you know how to hold the bow, place it on the string, and move the bow across all four strings while creating beautiful tones, it is time to learn a few basic bowings that form the foundation for most of the more complicated rhythms, or the variation of the duration of sound patterns in music. These basic bowings can be generalized: Long bows can create long notes and short bows can create short notes. You can find these basic bowings in the following three rhythmic exercises: "Four Long Notes, Mississippi-Stop-Stop," and Long-Tip-Tip-Long-Frog-Frog."

Here are the three rhythmic exercises (see the DVD):

- *Four Long Notes*—Place a straight bow on the A string near the frog of the bow, and move your bow using the entire length of the bow from the frog to the tip and back again, creating four long and smooth notes. Try this rhythmic exercise on all four strings.

- *Mississippi-Stop-Stop*—Place a straight bow on the A string near the middle of the bow, and move your bow in four short bow strokes centering around the middle and only using about 4–5 inches in bow length. This creates the rhythmic sound effect "Mis-si-ssi-ppi." To create the "Stop-Stop," simply pull a short down bow stroke, wait for a second, pull a short up bow stroke, and then wait for another second. Try this rhythmic exercise at the middle, tip, and frog of the bow.

- *Long-Tip-Tip-Long-Frog-Frog*—Place a straight bow on the A string near the frog of the bow and pull a long down bow using the entire length of the bow. Then play two short bow strokes at the tip of the bow (a little up bow, then a little down bow). Next, play a long up bow using the entire length of the bow. Finally, play two short bow strokes at the frog of the bow (a little down bow, then a little up bow). Try this rhythmic exercise on all four strings.

The speed of the bow plays a big role in terms of which part of the bow the violinist wants to use to manipulate the tone of each note. For instance, a violinist can play a long note using a small amount of bow in the upper half by pulling the bow very slowly to make the note last longer in time, creating a smooth gentle tone. A violinist can also play a short note using the whole bow by using a very fast and heavy bow to generate a sudden loud burst of tone. Experiment with the given rhythmic exercises, using different parts and lengths of the bow to discover various sound effects, and note that different strings can add an extra texture to your sound-effect collection, or *Repertoire*.

"Violin is a great instrument to play, because to play the violin correctly, you need lots of concentration. The violin has taught me how to concentrate to achieve my goals, even on non-musical challenges."

—Ruby, 10 years old

"I like discovering new musical notes on my violin, and playing my favorite songs with the bow."

—Colin, 10 years old

3

Fingering
Techniques

PICTURE YOURSELF FINGERING the strings of the violin with the greatest of ease and accuracy. This chapter will teach you how to place your left hand and move your fingers through the application of easy-to-use fingering tapes. You will also learn to interpret the musical ABCs, and apply that knowledge to finger every note on the violin being brought to life through your bow and pizzicato techniques. Your fingers will become quick and agile through an assortment of five-minute fingering exercises, and you will learn a new bowing technique called the *slur*.

Applying Fingering Tapes

THE VIOLIN IS A NON-FRETTED stringed instrument, and it is necessary to learn each note's precise location by identifying relative spacing between finger positions associated with the desired pitch. *Fingering tapes* are commonly used to help beginners learn the correct location of each note by guiding the placement of each finger on all four strings. My DVD students who purchase the Beginner series receive the appropriately colored fingering tapes within their DVD package; alternatively, you can purchase the 'Teacher's Choice Fingerboard Tapes" from most online music stores.

Here's how to identify the location for the proper placement of each fingering tape:

1. Tune the open strings using the SAT500 Seiko auto-chromatic tuner. Be sure to tune the strings to their appropriate pitch levels: G3, D4, A4, and E5.

2. Once the violin is in tune, place the violin on your lap, front side facing you, in preparation to pizzicato.

3. Use your right thumb to pizzicato the A string repeatedly through Step 4, so that the chromatic tuner can identify the pitch.

4. Find your 1st tape, B ♮, by pressing the left thumb on the A string and testing the pitch by moving the thumb in tiny increments along the string. The location of the 1st tape should be approximately one inch from the nut on the A string (see Figure 3.1).

Figure 3.1
Finding tape placements

5. Once you have located the exact spot on the A string that creates the pitch B ♮, you can use a pencil to mark on the fingerboard where the center of your finger intersects the A string (see Figure 3.2).

Figure 3.2
Pencil marking

6. Repeat steps 4 and 5 to find the next notes—Low 2 tape C ♮, High 2 tape C ♯, 3rd tape D ♮, and 4th tape E ♮"—all on the A string.

Spacing

There should be approximately one inch from the nut to the 1ˢᵗ tape B ♮, a half inch from the 1ˢᵗ tape to Low 2 tape C ♮, a half inch from the Low 2 tape to the High 2 tape C ♯, a half inch from the High 2 tape to the 3ʳᵈ tape D ♮, and one inch from the 3ʳᵈ tape to the 4ᵗʰ tape E ♮.

Here's how to apply the fingering tapes:

1. Lay the violin lengthwise on your lap with the scroll pointing away from you.

2. Peel the paper backing off a gold tape, being careful not to let the tape stick to itself.

3. Slide the tape, sticky side down, under the strings near the bridge, and then slide it up between the fingerboard and the strings until you arrive at the 1ˢᵗ pencil mark B ♮ (see Figure 3.3).

Figure 3.3
Sliding the tape under the strings

4. Before you attach the tape to the fingerboard, test the pitch by placing the center of your finger on the center of the tape while plucking the A string and using the chromatic tuner, and make sure that the tape is level, intersecting each string at a right angle.

5. Wrap the ends around the back of the neck, applying pressure as you rub the tape onto the wood of the neck to secure the attachment.

6. Repeat steps 2–5 to apply the remaining fingering tapes. Be sure to use the red tape for the Low 2 tape C ♮, and the rest of the gold tapes for the High 2 tape C ♯, 3ʳᵈ tape D ♮, and 4ᵗʰ tape E ♮ (see Figure 3.4).

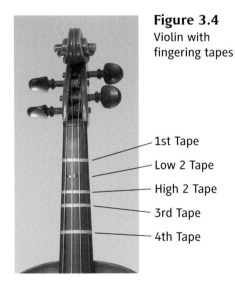

Figure 3.4
Violin with fingering tapes

1st Tape
Low 2 Tape
High 2 Tape
3rd Tape
4th Tape

Securing Tapes

If you want to secure the joining ends of the tapes on the back of the neck, you can apply clear Scotch tape or yellow masking tape to the back of the neck over the joining ends of the fingering tapes.

Setting the Hand

THIS SECTION SHOWS YOU how to properly place your hand on the neck of the violin and to accurately set each rounded fingertip on the strings through the easy-to-use fingering tapes. You will be shown how to set the *thumb* and the *palm line* onto the 1st tape, while keeping your fingers round and your wrist down.

Holding the Violin

The violin balances between your shoulder and the underside of your chin, allowing your fingers and wrist to move freely. Do not attempt to hold the weight of the violin with your left fingering hand. To reinforce good technique, while the violin is in playing position, drop your left hand down to your side once in a while to encourage the underside of your chin and shoulder to hold the weight of the violin properly.

Here's how to set the hand to the neck of the violin (see the DVD):

1. Place the violin in playing position, with no bow.

2. Apply the pad of your left thumb to the left side of the violin neck, directly on the side of the 1st fingering tape. The pad of the thumb will be the only part of the thumb that will actually touch the violin, and the remainder of the thumb should drop straight down (see Figure 3.5).

Figure 3.5
Thumb on 1st tape

3. The palm line and fingers will go on the right side of the violin neck, placing the palm line just behind the 1st fingering tape and level with the fingerboard (see Figure 3.6). Center the elbow comfortably under the violin and remember to keep the wrist flat, forming a straight line from the hand to the arm.

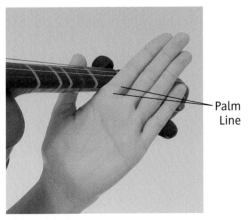

Palm Line

Figure 3.6
Palm line behind 1st tape

4. Rotate your hand and wrist clockwise, so that your hand is parallel to the neck of the violin, keeping the thumb straight and your wrist down (see Figure 3.7).

Figure 3.7
Hand parallel to the fingerboard

Round Fingers

When setting your fingers on the A string, be sure to set the tip of your fingers on the center of each tape. This will encourage your fingers to have a round arch through all joints. To set your fingers correctly, you will need to trim your fingernails short, so that the nail will not interfere with pitch production.

Here's how to set your fingers on the strings (see the DVD):

1. Place the violin in playing position and set your thumb and palm line in the fingering position, no bow.

2. Place your 1st finger on the 1st tape B ♮, very round on the tip of the finger by the fingernail and almost uncomfortably pulled backward within the hand, forming the shape of a tight square from the three sides of the finger and the string (see Figure 3.8).

Figure 3.8
Setting the 1st finger

3. The 2nd finger can be placed on either the red Low 2 tape C ♮ or the gold High 2 tape C ♯, according to the naturals or sharps in a song (see Figure 3.9).

Figure 3.9
Setting the 2nd finger

4. Set the 3rd finger on the 3rd tape D ♮, round on the tip of the finger by the fingernail. Be sure to relax the squeezing pressure from your thumb and keep your wrist down (see Figure 3.10).

Figure 3.10
Setting the 3rd finger

5. Set the 4th finger on the 4th tape E ♮, round on the tip of the finger by the fingernail (see Figure 3.11).

Figure 3.11
Setting the 4th finger

6. Repeat steps 2–5, setting the fingers on each tape on all four strings while keeping the thumb down and the wrist flat and straight.

Thumb Pressure

As you practice setting each finger, try to release the squeezing pressure on the thumb by tapping the thumb on the side of the neck as you set fingers on the tapes. This will encourage a relaxed hand and good technique. The thumb should be used as an anchor, keeping the hand in one location, by simply resting on the side of the violin neck.

"Violin is a great instrument to play, because to play the violin correctly, you need lots of concentration. The violin has taught me how to concentrate to achieve my goals, even on non-musical challenges."

—Ruby, 10 years old

Moving the Fingers

THERE ARE A FEW WONDERFUL five-minute fingering exercises to practice daily so that your fingers can adjust to the strings and become flexible. These fingering exercises include the Finger Bounce, Finger Strike, Cross Over and Hop, and Elbow Swing. When practicing these exercises, take your time and let your hand truly learn each new concept.

Finger Bounce

The Finger Bounce exercise will teach the hand exactly how little pressure and energy it takes to move a tiny string onto and off of the fingerboard. Your tone quality comes from both the solid connection between the tip of your finger pressing the string onto the fingerboard and the angle of your bow to your strings. You will need to perfect both techniques to achieve the best tone quality from your violin for rich warm singing tones.

Here's how to practice the Finger Bounce technique (see the DVD):

1. Place the violin in playing position and set your thumb and palm line in the fingering position, no bow.

2. Set your 1st finger round on the tip of the finger on the 1st tape B ♮, on the A string.

3. Lightly bounce the tip of your 1st finger on the string, onto and off of the fingerboard in small motions, never letting the finger leave the string.

4. Try to relax your entire hand, and decrease the amount of pressure and energy used from your hand for every bounce.

5. Repeat steps 2–4 by slowly adding each finger on all the gold tapes, until all four fingers are bouncing on the string effortlessly at the same time. If you find yourself squeezing the neck of the violin between your thumb and palm line, simply remove your thumb completely from the violin and continue the Finger Bounce exercise so that your hand will learn how to set the fingers with only the up and down motion of the fingers' knuckles.

"Mrs. Seidel is the BEST violin teacher ever! Even though the violin can be difficult at times, she always makes it seem easy and fun. She expects the very best of us at each lesson, but has a great sense of humor as well. For instance, one time we were snapping beans, while waiting for our lesson and one of the beans flew through the air and fell right through the F–hole of the violin! What are the odds of that?! Mrs. Seidel just cracked up as she skillfully picked the bean out of the violin and said, 'This is definitely a first for me!'"

—Claire, Kalin, Payton, and Emma

Finger Strike

Hand and finger memorization is critical when it comes to mastering the violin. The *Finger Strike* exercise will quickly enable your fingers to learn the exact spot on every string for each note by forcibly striking your fingers on the center of each tape. This motion will teach your fingers where the tapes are quickly and effectively, without the bad habit of scooting or wiggling a finger on the string until you eventually reach a correct note.

Here's how to practice the Finger Strike technique (see the DVD):

1. Set the violin, hand, and fingers in playing position, no bow.

2. Forcibly strike your 1st finger down on the A string, creating a thumping sound from the strike impact of your finger tip suddenly hitting the string against the fingerboard.

3. Hold your finger on the exact location where it hits the string and see how close you are to the center of the desired tape.

4. Try again several times until you can strike your finger perfectly on the center of the desired tape.

5. Apply steps 2–4 for each separate finger, striking only one finger at a time.

Cross Over and Hop

One characteristic of a proper fingering technique involves the ability to hold fingers down while crossing over and hopping other fingers on the strings. This technique of holding fingers down allows a violinist to use finger relativity to judge correct spacing for precise intonation.

Here's how to practice the Cross Over and Hop technique (see the DVD):

1. Set the violin, hand, and fingers in playing position, no bow.

2. Hold your 1st finger B round on the tip of the finger, on the A string.

3. Use your red Low 2 tape to set the 2nd finger on the A string for C ♮.

4. Hold the 1st finger B on the A string, while you "cross over and hop" your Low 2 on the D string, A string, E string, and then back to the A string (see Figure 3.12).

Figure 3.12
Holding 1st, Low 2 on D string, A string, and E string

5. Repeat this exercise while holding your 1st finger on each string while taking turns crossing over and hopping your Low 2, 3rd, and 4th fingers to the surrounding strings.

Remember

The purpose of this exercise is to judge the distance between each finger in order to improve hand memorization and intonation.

Elbow Swing

The Elbow Swing allows your fingers to keep the same hand shape, finger roundness, and finger spacing for every string, which makes achieving correct intonation easier.

Wrist

Keep your hand and wrist straight with your arm while you practice swinging your elbow. Do not allow your wrist to collapse or to have a sideways curve either to the right or left when you move your fingers to the upper strings.

Here's how to practice the Elbow Swing technique (see the DVD):

1. Set the violin, hand, and fingers in playing position, no bow.

2. Hover all four fingers over the A string gold tapes (see Figure 3.13).

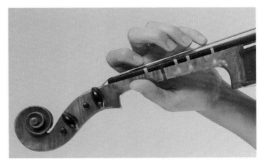

Figure 3.13
Hovering all four fingers

3. Keep all fingers round and the hand position still.

4. Swing your elbow from the left (see Figure 3.14) to the right side (see Figure 3.15), under the violin.

Left Elbow Swing

Figure 3.14
Left elbow swing

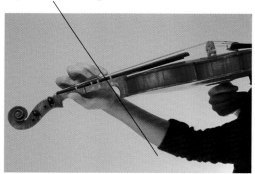

Right Elbow Swing

Figure 3.15
Right elbow swing

5. This swinging motion automatically moves your fingers from the E string to the G string, without adjusting your finger's roundness or finger spacing.

Anticipate String Change

To perfect your technique, you need to anticipate the string change through the swing of your elbow. For example, if you are moving to an upper string, you will need to anticipate the string change by swinging your elbow to the left side of the violin before the actual string change occurs with your fingers, creating a smooth transition from one string to another with a constant slow swing of the elbow. You can also apply this concept when moving to a lower string on the violin by swinging your elbow to the right side of the violin before the actual string change occurs with your fingers.

"When our daughter began violin with Mrs. Seidel, she was an extremely shy 11–year old who played her violin timidly. Within months of working with Mrs. Seidel, she began to play the violin with emotion, enthusiasm, and confidence, which has spilled over into her other activities. We are very appreciative of the work that Mrs. Seidel has done with our daughter."

—Anita and Leslie

Musical ABCs

THE MUSICAL ABCs CONSIST of eight notes: ABCDEFG. This pattern repeats itself to fill all pitch ranges of notes, and an eight-note series is called an *octave*. That is why you need to tune your strings to a specific pitch level; for instance, G3 is the 3rd G octave in music.

To add color or different moods to a song, a composer can adjust a note three ways: flat (♭), natural (♮), and sharp (♯). When musicians talk about notes, they must be specific in naming a note with its sign, like A (♭) or A (♯). Every note is natural unless stated otherwise by a flat sign or a sharp sign, so it is common to see a note without a symbol, which automatically means perform the note as a natural.

Stepwise

A note changes its name by moving stepwise from a flat (♭), to a natural (♮), and then to a sharp (♯), or it can move in reverse from a sharp (♯), to a natural (♮), and then to a flat (♭). Notes cannot skip directly from flats to sharps or from sharps to flats without first moving to a natural (see Figure 3.16).

Figure 3.16
Flat, natural, and sharp chart

Finger Patterns

FINGER PATTERNS SHOW YOU where each flat, natural, and sharp is for each finger on all four strings, like a road map that helps simplify your finger movements. There are four finger patterns to learn: High 2, Low 2, Low 1, and High 3. Each finger pattern contains a certain combination of fingers; for example, the High 2 finger pattern allows the violinist to concentrate only on the gold tape notes on all four strings.

Here's how to practice the High 2 finger pattern with pizzicato (see Figure 3.17):

1. Set the violin, hand, and fingers in playing position, and swing the elbow to the right, under the violin, so that your fingers can reach the G string.

2. Prepare to play the open G string by lifting your fingers off the string.

3. Say the note name "G ♮" out loud.

4. Pizzicato the note by plucking the open G string.

5. Continue through the process of setting each finger, saying the note name with its appropriate symbol out loud, and then pizzicato the appropriate string to play all of the notes in the High 2 finger pattern.

Changing Strings

When going up a finger pattern, release all four fingers and move both the hand and the plucking finger to the next string higher. When going down a finger pattern, move your hand and plucking finger to the next string lower and set down your 1st, 2nd, 3rd, and 4th fingers to continue on the new string.

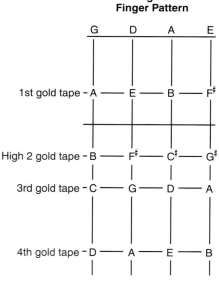

Figure 3.17
High 2 finger pattern and chart

Here's how to practice all four finger patterns with the bow (see the DVD):

1. Set the violin, hand, and fingers in playing position, and swing the elbow to the right, under the violin so that your fingers can reach the G string. At the frog, place a straight bow on the G string.

2. Set the finger, or prepare to play an open string by lifting the fingers off the string.

3. Say the note name with its appropriate symbol out loud.

4. Bow the note by using your full range of motion in both a long, smooth, down bow, and then repeat the note with a long smooth, up bow.

5. Repeat steps 2–4.

Low 2 Finger Pattern

The Low 2 finger pattern is similar to the High 2 finger pattern, except that the 2nd finger is placed on the red Low 2 tape. When practicing the Low 2 finger pattern, the lowered 2nd finger will touch the 1st finger. Be sure to reach the 3rd finger past the High 2 tape so that the 3rd finger can be properly placed onto the 3rd tape (see Figure 3.18).

Sound Problems

Do not worry about squeaks and crunches; just fix as you go. If you encounter a problem with a certain note, check the bow speed and pressure, and make sure the bow is on the desired string and that the tip of the finger is pressing the string down with solid contact to the fingerboard. Don't forget to keep your wrist down and fingers round, and do a bow hold check occasionally: "thumb bent, pinky round, shoulders down and relaxed."

Low 2 Finger Pattern

	G	D	A	E
1st gold tape	A	E	B	F♯
Low 2 red tape	B♭	F$^{(♮)}$	C$^{(♮)}$	G$^{(♮)}$
3rd gold tape	C	G	D	A
4th gold tape	D	A	E	B

Figure 3.18
Low 2 finger pattern and chart

Low 1
Finger Pattern

	G	D	A	E
Low 1 –	A♭	E♭	B♭	F⁽♮⁾
Low 2 red tape –	B♭	F⁽♮⁾	C⁽♮⁾	G⁽♮⁾
3rd gold tape –	C	G	D	A
4th gold tape –	D	A	E	B

Figure 3.19
Low 1 finger pattern and chart

Low 1 Finger Pattern

The Low 1 finger pattern pulls your 1st finger back between the 1st tape and the nut of the violin; the 2nd, 3rd, and 4th fingers are similar to the Low 2 finger pattern. Make sure to set the palm line behind the 1st tape and pull the 1st finger back uncomfortably, while the rest of the fingers stay round and comfortable on the tapes. If it is hard to reach your 4th tape, scoot your palm line closer to the 1st tape, giving your hand a better central location to finger each note (see Figure 3.19).

High 3
Finger Pattern

	G	D	A	E
1st gold tape –	A	E	B	F♯
High 2 gold tape –	B	F♯	C♯	G♯
High 3 –	C♯	G♯	D♯	A♯
4th gold tape –	D	A	E	B

High 3 Finger Pattern

The High 3 finger pattern is similar to the High 2 finger pattern, except that the 3rd finger is placed in the middle between the 3rd tape and 4th tape. When practicing the High 3 finger pattern, the raised 3rd finger will touch the 4th finger (see Figure 3.20).

Figure 3.20
High 3 finger pattern and chart

Reading Straight Across

TO UNDERSTAND THE ORDER of the notes on every string, I recommend the *Straight Across* technique. This technique improves your ability to correlate the notes to each individual tape by reading and reciting the tape notes straight across all four strings from the G string to the E string.

Here's how to read the notes straight across:

1. Name all of the opens (G, D, A, and E).

2. Name all of the 1ˢᵗ tape notes (A, E, B, and F ♯).

3. Name all of the Low 2s (B ♭, F, C, and G).

4. Name all of the High 2s (B, F ♯, C ♯, and G ♯).

5. Name all of the 3ʳᵈ tape notes (C, G, D, and A).

6. Name all of the 4ᵗʰ tape notes (D, A, E, and B).

7. Name all of the Low 1s (A ♭, E ♭, B ♭, and F)

8. Name all of the High 3s (C ♯, G ♯, D ♯, and A ♯).

9. Once you can easily recite the note names straight across from memory, hold your violin in playing position and either pizzicato or bow straight across while saying each note name out loud.

Fifths

Notice that the notes repeat in a pattern as you read straight across. The pattern is called 5ths, or every five notes (A, bcd, and E). If you can pick up on the pattern, it will simplify the road map of the violin notes. The order of the 5th is as follows: A, E, B, F, C, G, D, and then back to A.

"My teacher helps me play the violin well, and I love the candy after the lesson!"

—Sujay, 8 years old

Finger-Pattern Slurs

T HE LAST STEP TO MASTERING full
mobility on the violin is a little exercise called
Finger-Pattern Slurs. It combines your finger
patterns isolated on a single string with a new
bowing technique called the slur. A *slur* is when
you play two or more notes in a single bow stoke.

Here's how to slur notes together:

1. Set the violin, hand, and fingers in playing
   position, and start on the A string with your
   bow at the frog.

2. Slur two notes: Use half of the bow for an
   open A and the other half for 1st finger B by
   pulling a smooth and continuous down bow
   (∏). When you arrive to the middle of the
   bow just set your 1st finger on the string
   without stopping the bow (see Figure 3.21).

3. Try the new bowing technique up bow (V)
   by starting with the 1st finger B and lifting it
   up to play open A (see Figure 3.22).

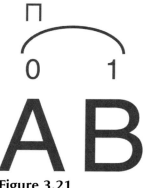

Figure 3.21
Two-note slur, down bow

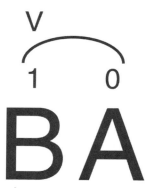

Figure 3.22
Two-note slur, up bow

4. Slur three notes: Divide your bow in thirds and play open A, 1st finger B, and High 2 C♯, all in the same down bow. Reverse the fingerings on the up bow, starting with the High 2, 1st finger, and then open A (see Figure 3.23).

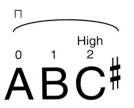 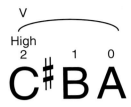

Figure 3.23
Three-note slur, down and up bow

5. Slur four notes: Divide your bow in fourths playing open A, 1st finger B, High 2 C♯), and 3rd finger D, all slurred down bow. Reverse the fingering to go up bow, starting with the 3rd finger, High 2, 1st finger, and then open A (see Figure 3.24).

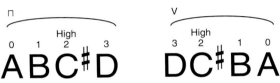

Figure 3.24
Four-note slur, down and up bow

6. Slur five notes: With a slow down bow, slur the open A through 4th finger, and reverse the fingerings going up bow (see Figure 3.25).

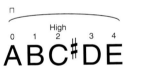 

Figure 3.25
Five-note slur, down and up bow

You are now ready to practice the Finger-Pattern Slur exercises, which are designed to teach your fingers to quickly transition between different finger patterns while accurately setting your fingers on each tape on a single string. These exercises will help you master speed and agility of your fingers and obtain greater control over bow techniques. The goal here is to maintain good tone quality from the tip to frog of your bow while perfecting the bow-saving techniques needed to perform five notes in a single bow stroke slur.

Here's how to practice the finger-pattern slurs (see the DVD):

1. Set the violin, hand, and fingers in playing position, and start on the A string with your bow at the frog.

2. On the A string, slur a High 3 finger pattern. Repeat this finger-pattern slur until your fingers perfectly strike every tape comfortably (see Figure 3.26).

3. On the A string, slur a High 2 finger pattern. Repeat this finger-pattern slur until your fingers perfectly strike every tape comfortably (see Figure 3.27).

4. On the A string, slur a Low 2 finger pattern. Repeat this finger-pattern slur until your fingers perfectly strike every tape comfortably (see Figure 3.28).

5. On the A string, slur a Low 1 finger pattern. Repeat this finger-pattern slur until your fingers perfectly strike every tape comfortably (see Figure 3.29).

6. Repeat this exercise on all four strings.

Figure 3.26
High 3, down and up bow

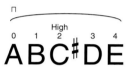
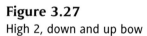
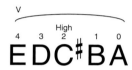

Figure 3.27
High 2, down and up bow

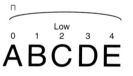
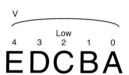

Figure 3.28
Low 2, down and up bow

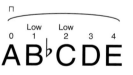

Figure 3.29
Low 1, down and up bow

Check Good Technique

Be sure to swing your elbow so that your fingers can reach each new string, and remember to check for good technique. Fingering hand: wrist down, fingers round, and palm line right behind 1st tape. Bow hand: thumb bent, pinky round, shoulders down and relaxed.

Music
Theory

PICTURE YOURSELF READING SHEET MUSIC of
your favorite song and being able to fully understand all
of the symbols and note names on the staff. As you are
about to play the first measure of your song, you glance over at
the key signature to figure out which notes are sharp or flat, and
at the same time you glance at the time signature to understand
the basic count and rhythmic pulse of the beat. Then you read
the first few notes on the page, set your fingers and your bow
on the strings, and within a few moments you are performing
your favorite song on the violin. This chapter will teach you all
of this and more, through easy-to-follow exercises that are
arranged in a progression of skill levels that will add to your
gained knowledge.

Reading Notes

THE ABILITY TO READ MUSIC opens an unlimited world of sheet music for a violinist. Once you know how to read music, you can look at any song for a few seconds and instantly figure out how to perform it perfectly. Reading music can unshackle a violinist from constant practicing, memorization, and from a limited song repertoire.

Note Names

In music, notes are divided into line notes and space notes. The placement of the note head on the staff shows the musician its name and which string it relates to on the violin. There are a few easy sayings to help a musician learn the note names on the staff, but the fastest way to read music is to simply learn which space or line goes with each note. For example, second space A; whenever you see a note on the second space of the staff, it will always be the note A.

Line notes

Line notes sit on the five lines of a staff. You can tell a note is a line note by observing that the line of the staff cuts straight through the center of the note head. There is an easy saying to help you memorize the order of the line notes from the bottom to the top of the staff: **E**very **G**ood **B**oy **D**oes **F**ine (see Figure 4.1).

Here are the five line notes to memorize:

  Top line F (see Figure 4.2)

Figure 4.2
Top line F

  Fourth line D (see Figure 4.3)

Figure 4.3
Fourth line D

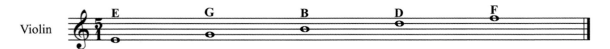

Figure 4.1
Line notes

✎ Middle Line B (see Figure 4.4)

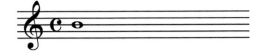

Figure 4.4
Middle line B

✎ Second line G (see Figure 4.5)

Figure 4.5
Second line G

✎ First line E (see Figure 4.6)

Figure 4.6
First line E

Space Notes

Space notes sit on the four spaces of a staff. You can tell a note is a space note by observing that the lines of the staff are above and below the note head. There is an easy word that can help you memorize the order of the space notes from the bottom to the top of the staff: *FACE* (see Figure 4.7)

Here are the four space notes to memorize:

✎ Fourth space E (see Figure 4.8)

Figure 4.8
Fourth space E

✎ Third space C (see Figure 4.9)

Figure 4.9
Third space C

✎ Second space A (see Figure 4.10)

Figure 4.10
Second space A

Figure 4.7
Space notes

First space F (see Figure 4.11)

Figure 4.11
First space F

Ledger Lines

A *ledger line* is a short line below or above the staff that continues the notes names beyond the staff's five lines. A beginning violinist needs to memorize only two ledger lines below and above the staff (see Figure 4.12), but when you become an advanced violinist, there are many notes on the ledger lines above the staff you'll use on an every-day basis.

Here are the ledger lines below the staff to memorize:

Below the staff D (see Figure 4.13)

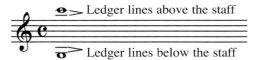
Ledger lines above the staff
Ledger lines below the staff

Figure 4.13
Below the staff D

First ledger line C (see Figure 4.14)

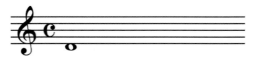

Figure 4.14
First ledger line C

Below the first ledger line B (see Figure 4.15)

Figure 4.15
Below the first ledger line B

Second ledger line A (see Figure 4.16)

Figure 4.16
Second ledger line A

Below the second ledger line G (see Figure 4.17)

Figure 4.17
Below the second ledger line G

Here are the ledger lines above the staff to memorize:

- Second ledger line C (see Figure 4.18)

Figure 4.18
Second ledger line C

- Above the first ledger line B (see Figure 4.19)

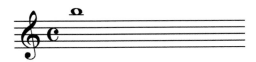

Figure 4.19
Above the first ledger line B

- On the first ledger line A (see Figure 4.20)

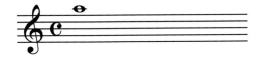

Figure 4.20
On the first ledger line A

- Above the staff G (see Figure 4.21)

Figure 4.21
Above the staff G

"When I first started playing the violin, I did not like practicing, but as I learned more, I began to like how I sounded and started to enjoy practicing. I've made amazing friends through the violin and orchestra, and I have many fond memories of competitions, concerts, and recitals. I've also developed a great respect for anyone who plays an instrument. Playing the violin, and any instrument for that matter, takes a massive amount of dedication and hard work. There's a sense of accomplishment that I love, when you've mastered a piece or you've done well at a recital. I'll be the first to tell you that playing the violin is not easy, but it is definitely worth it."

—Lisa, 14 years old

Violin Strings

Each of the four violin strings is assigned four notes on the staff, with a repeating note 4th finger. You can now compare side to side how the finger patterns correlate with the notes on the staff.

The E string comparison is shown in Figures 4.22 and 4.23.

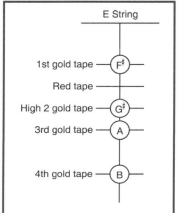

Figure 4.22
E string finger pattern

The A string comparison is shown in Figures 4.24 and 4.25.

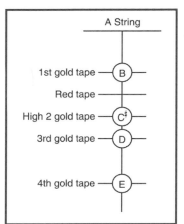

Figure 4.24
A string finger pattern

Figure 4.23
E string note names

Figure 4.25
A string note names

The D string comparison is shown in Figures 4.26 and 4.27.

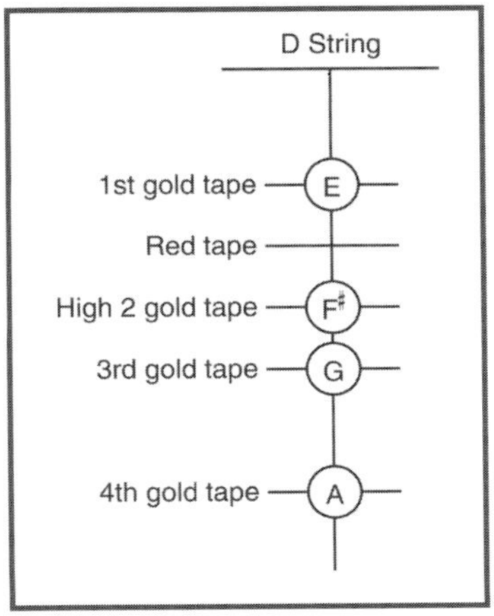

The G string comparison is shown in Figures 4.28 and 4.29.

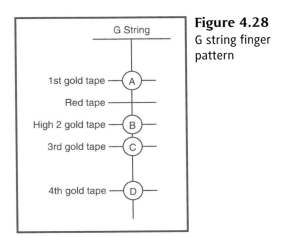

Figure 4.26
D string finger pattern

Figure 4.28
G string finger pattern

Figure 4.27
D string note names

Figure 4.29
G string note names

Octaves

An *octave* is a series of eight notes. In music you can have the same note repeated an octave higher, for example the note G is played as Open G, 3rd finger G on the D string, and Low 2 G on the E string. It is a good idea to learn where each octave is on the violin so you can better understand which G on the staff correlates to which G on the violin (see Figure 4.30).

Reading Sheet Music

Sheet music is made up of a few basic symbols that organize a song into easy-to-understand sections. Once you understand how to read sheet music, you can effortlessly learn a new song anytime and anywhere.

Take a look at Figure 4.31 for an illustration on how to read sheet music:

Figure 4.30
Violin octaves

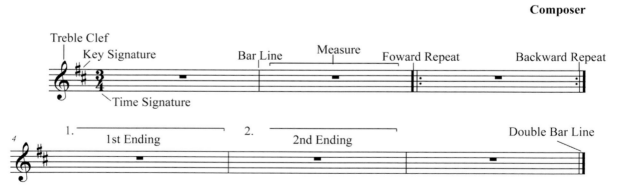

Figure 4.31
Sheet music symbols

74

- *Song title*—Top center of the page; gives the name of the song.

- *Composer*—Top-right side of the page; gives the name of the person who wrote the song.

- *Treble clef*—The first symbol to the extreme left of the staff; indicates violin sheet music.

- *Key signature*—The second symbol to the extreme left of the staff; explains the set rules of the sharps, naturals, or flats for certain notes in the song.

- *Time signature*—The third symbol to the extreme left of the staff; explains how many beats are in a measure, and which note value gets the beat.

- *Bar line*—The slim black line that separates every measure.

- *Repeat symbols*—Two vertical dots next to a slim black line and a thick black line; indicates to repeat the section you just played.

- *First ending and second ending*—A repeating section with a number 1 above a measure and a number 2 above the next measure, meaning on the first time performing the music play measure number 1, repeat the section, and on the second time performing the music, skip over the measure number 1 and play measure number 2.

- *Double bar line*—A slim black line next to a thick black line, meaning the end of the song.

Reading Note Names Exercises

You can now test your knowledge of reading note names and performing them on the violin. Each new exercise is a progression of skill level, so please practice each exercise until you feel comfortable with the material before moving to the next exercise.

Here are the reading note names exercises:

- *Open*—Learn how to read the Open strings of the violin, as shown in Figure 4.32. Set your violin and bow in playing position and your left hand on the right shoulder of the violin. Use your string roll technique to roll to each new string as you bow and say out loud each string name. While bowing, use long smooth bows at a slow pace.

"Violin makes me and my family members happy. My shining moment is when I get a hundred on my grade in my private lessons. I feel great and love the music I play as a violinist. The violin taught me to be strong by standing straight and holding the violin properly. I also selected the violin because I like music and like playing the violin."

—Jimmy, 8 years old

Figure 4.32
Open strings

🌸 *1st – 4th fingers on each string*—Learn how to read each finger on the separate four strings of the violin, as illustrated in Figure 4.33. Set your violin, bow, and fingering hand in playing position. Play and finger the notes while you say each note name out loud. Notice that each string uses the same pattern of fingers. While bowing, use long smooth bows at a slow pace.

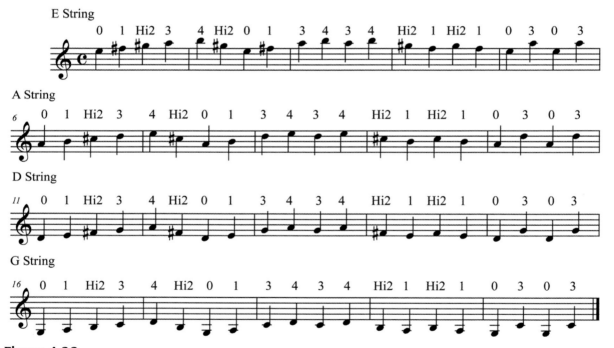

Figure 4.33
1st–4th fingers on each string

🍀 *Intervals*—The distance between two notes. Learn how to identify *step-wise* notes from skipping notes (see Figure 4.34). Set your violin, bow, and fingering hand in playing position. Play and finger the notes while you say each note name out loud. Notice that the *skips on spaces* use the opens, 2nd, and 4th fingers, where as the *skips on lines* use the 1st and 3rd fingers. While bowing, use long smooth bows at a slow pace.

🍀 *Mixtures*—Learn how to master reading note names and performing them on the violin (see Figure 4.35). Set your violin, bow, and fingering hand in playing position. Play and finger the notes while you say each note name out loud. For extra help, you can always refer to previous examples. While bowing, use long smooth bows at a slow pace.

Figure 4.34
Intervals

Figure 4.35
Mixtures

Key Signatures

THE *KEY SIGNATURE* SETS THE starting rules for each song. A composer can choose to make a certain note into a sharp or a flat, depending on what ambiance the composer is trying to create. For example, if there is only one sharp (F♯) in the key signature, then all octave Fs must automatically be performed as an F♯ through out the entire song.

The Order of Sharps and Flats

There is a specific order of sharps and flats that all composers must follow when writing a song. This makes reading music and remembering the key signature much easier for the musician, because in every song in the world, written in any year, and from any part of the world, if it has one sharp in the key signature, the sharp will always be F♯.

Here's the order from one sharp to four sharps in the key signature:

✒ F♯ (see Figure 4.36)

Figure 5.36
One sharp

✒ F♯, C♯ (see Figure 4.37)

Figure 4.37
Two sharps

✒ F♯, C♯, G♯ (see Figure 4.38)

Figure 4.38
Three sharps

✒ F♯, C♯, G♯, D♯ (see Figure 4.39)

Figure 4.39
Four sharps

Here's the order from one flat to four flats in the key signature:

✒ B♭ (see Figure 4.40)

Figure 4.40
One flat

✒ B♭, E♭ (see Figure 4.41)

Figure 4.41
Two flats

🎵 B♭, E♭, A♭ (see Figure 4.42)

Figure 4.42
Three flats

🎵 B♭, E♭, A♭, D♭ (see Figure 4.43)

Figure 4.43
Four flats

Key Signature Names

A *key signature name* is like a family name, and how many sharps/ flats are in the key signature is like how many people are in the family. For example, the key signature *A Major* has three people in its family, their names are F♯, C♯, and G♯.

Finding the Sharp Key Signature Names

Look at the last sharp in the key signature and go up a half step (fingers touching) to the next note in the musical ABCs. For example, if the last sharp is F♯, the key name is G Major, and if you have two sharps, ♯ and C♯, the key name is D Major.

Finding the Flat Key Signature Names

There is a different method to correlating the number of flats in a key to a flat key signature name. First, memorize the word "F-B♭ E♭A♭D♭," which is the order of the flat key signature names. If a key has one flat, it will correlate to the first letter of the memorized word, giving it the key name of F Major. For example, a key that has two flats has a key name of B♭ Major, a key that has three flats has a key name of E♭ Major, and a key that has four flats has the key name of A♭ Major.

Circle of 5th

The *Circle of 5th* is a key-signature chart that shows the entire list of major and minor key names with the number of sharps or flats they share (see Figure 4.44). A minor key is like the evil twin of a major key; they both can have the same amount of sharps or flats in the key signature, but the minor has a twist in the notes by changing a specific note into a natural or a sharp.

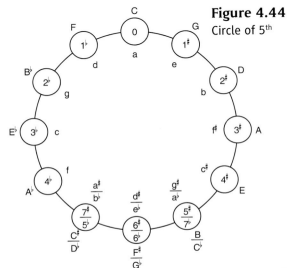

Figure 4.44
Circle of 5th

79

Violin Tapes

You can use your tapes on the violin to help memorize the order of the sharps and flats of the key signatures by following the notes from string to string on the Low 1 tape for flats and the High 2 tape for sharps.

Here's how to follow your fingering tapes:

🎵 *Sharps*—Follow the notes using your High 2 tape from the G string going up to the E string (see Figure 4.45). B is the first High 2 in the key of C Major. F♯ is the second High 2 in the key of G Major. C♯ is the fourth High 2 in the key of A Major.

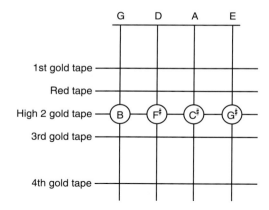

Figure 4.45
Sequence of sharps in High 2

🎵 *Flats*—Follow the notes using your Low 1 tape from the E string going down to the G string (see Figure 4.46). F is the first Low 1 in the key of C Major. B♭ is the second Low 1 in the key of F Major. E♭ is the third Low 1 in the key of B♭ Major. A♭ is the fourth Low 1 in the key of E♭ Major.

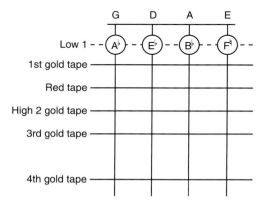

Figure 4.46
Sequence of flats on Low 1

Scales

A scale prepares your mind and your fingers to perform a song in a certain key signature by allowing you to play every note on the violin to find out which fingers are low and which fingers are high. It is also a good idea to warm up on a scale before you start your practice session; this allows your fingers to move on all four strings and allows you to stretch out your bow arm by using the full length of the bow.

There are four rules when playing a scale:

- ✍ **Begin and end on the key name. If the key name is G Major then your first and last note is G.**

- ✍ **Play every note in order of the alphabet. Use your 4th fingers instead of your Opens. G Major Scale: G, A, B, C, D, E, F, G.**

- ✍ **Follow the key signature. Play every note a natural except for what is sharp or flat in the key. G Major: G♮, A♮, B♮, C♮, D♮, E♮, F♯, G♮.**

- ✍ **Play in octaves. One octave G Major is every note from Open G through 3rd finger G on the D string. Two octave G Major is every note from Open G through Low 2 G on the E string.**

Sharp Scales

A *sharp scale* is a scale with only sharps in the key signature. A violinist normally performs scales up to three sharps: G Major, D Major, and A Major. Each new scale is a progression of skill level, so please practice each scale until you feel completely comfortable with the material before moving to the next scale.

Here are the three sharp scales:

- ✍ *G Major*—One sharp: F♯ (see Figure 4.47).

- ✍ *D Major*—Two sharps: F♯ and C♯ (see Figure 4.48).

- ✍ *A Major*—Three sharps: F♯, C♯, and G♯ (see Figure 4.49).

Figure 4.47
G Major two-octaves scale

Figure 4.48
D Major one-octave scale

Figure 4.49
A Major two-octave scale

Flat Scales

A *flat scale* is a scale with only flats in the key signature. A violinist normally performs scales up to three flats: F Major, B♭ Major, and E♭ Major. Each new scale is a progression of skill level, so please practice each scale until you feel completely comfortable with the material before moving to the next scale.

Here are the three flat scales:

- *F Major*—One flat: B♭ (see Figure 4.50).
- *B♭ Major*—Two flats: B♭ and E♭ (see Figure 4.51).
- *E♭ Major*—Three flats: B♭, E♭, and A♭ (see Figure 4.52).

Figure 4.50

F Major one-octave scale

Figure 4.51

B♭ Major two-octave scale

Figure 4.52

E♭ Major one-octave scale

Key Signature Specialties

There are some exceptions to the rules when it comes to following the given key signature. Written within the music, a composer can change a flat, natural, or a sharp for a particular note that can last a length of a single measure, or the composer can change a flat, natural, or a sharp for a particular note that can last a length of the song by changing the entire key signature.

Here's a few of the key-signature specialties:

- *Natural scale*—There is only one natural scale, C Major. Every note in this scale will be performed as a natural note (see Figure 4.53).

- *Accidentals*—An *accidental* is a sharp, natural, or flat that is added next to a note within a measure that is not part of the key signature. The accidental will affect the same note through the entire measure until the bar line, and the next new measure will default all notes back to the key signature (see Figure 4.54).

- *Key change*—A *key change* is when a key signature changes from one key to another key within the same song. In music, a song can stay in the same key or change keys several times. When a composer changes key signatures, he or she must correct the old notes with natural signs before adding the new sharp or flat signs (see Figure 4.55).

Figure 4.53
C Major one-octave scale

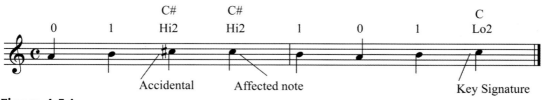

Figure 4.54
Accidentals

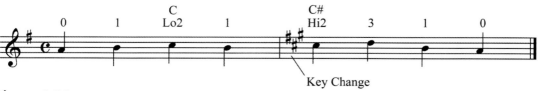

Figure 4.55
Key change

Time Signatures

THE *TIME SIGNATURE* IS REPRESENTED by two numbers—a top number showing how many beats per measure, and a bottom number showing which value of note gets the beat. The time signature tells the musician how to count the song, and the overall feeling of the song by pairing the main beat in two (ONE-two, ONE-two), or by pairing the main beat in three (ONE-two-three, ONE-two-three).

Beats per Measure

In music, the top number of the time signature reveals the two different types of time signatures: *simple time* refers to the top numbers 2, 3, and 4, and *compound time* refers to the top numbers 6, 9, and 12. With a simple time signature, what you see is what you get. If there is a 2 at the top, then there are two beats per measure; a 3 at the top receives three beats per measure; and a 4 at the top receives four beats per measure. Compound time signatures work differently. In this case, you need to divide the top by a triplet (or by 3) to determine how many beats per measure. Using this simple math, a 6 at the top receives three beats per measure; a 9 at the

top receives three beats per measure; and a 12 at the top receives four beats per measure. Now that you know that both time signatures have two, three, and four beats per measure, you need to know that simple time divides each beat into two syllables, whereas compound time divides each beat into three syllables, giving the music two very different feelings in rhythm.

Here are the two types of time signatures:

- *Simple*—The top numbers are 2, 3, and 4. Respectively, the numbers of beats per measure are 2, 3, and 4 (see Figure 4.56). Each beat is divided into two syllables; for example the top number 4 is counted with four beats "1&, 2&, 3&, 4&."

- *Compound*—The top numbers are 6, 9, and 12. Respectively, the numbers of beats per measure are 2, 3, and 4 (see Figure 4.57). Each beat is divided into three syllables, for example the top number 12 is counted with four beats "1-la-le, 2-la-le, 3-la-le, 4-la-le."

Figure 4.56
Simple time signature

Figure 4.57
Compound time signature

Rhythm Charts

The *rhythm chart* shows each value of note and how it breaks down into smaller note values in simple and compound time. In music, for each different value of note there is a matching value of rest (or a beat of silence). Figure 4.58 shows the simple rhythm chart and Figure 4.59 shows the compound rhythm chart.

Rhythm Exercises

A musician's best friend is the metronome; this simple yet effect device can turn a novice into a true rhythmic expert. When working with a metronome, it is very important to begin your note at the exact instant the beat "clicks." Do not start early and play your note before the click, and do not play your note late as a reaction to the click, but try to anticipate the beat so that you can arrive at the exact moment of time with the click of the metronome.

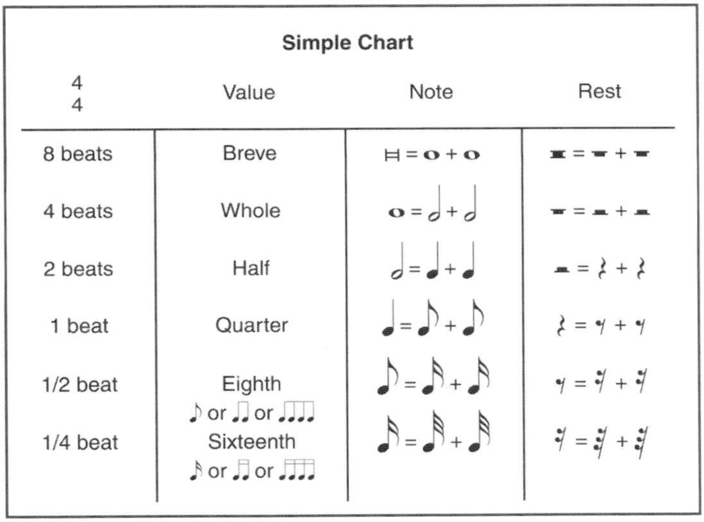

Figure 4.58
Simple rhythm chart

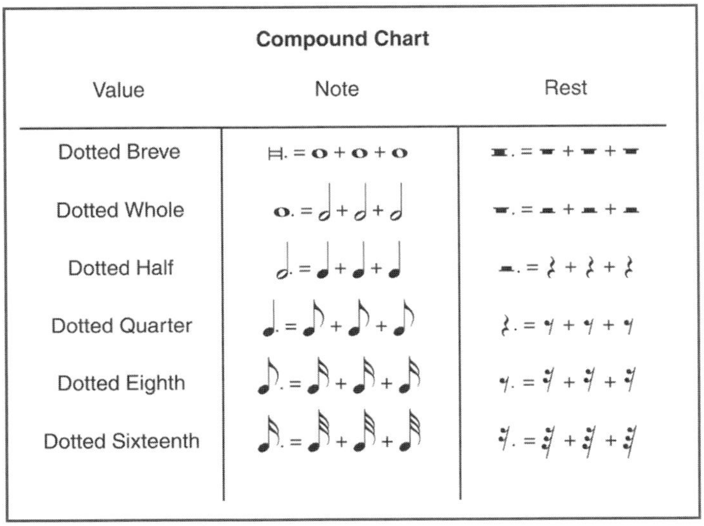

Figure 4.59
Compound rhythm chart

Each new exercise is a progression of skill level, so please practice each exercise until you feel completely comfortable with the material before moving to the next exercise.

Here are the rhythm exercises:

- *Beat Notes*—This exercise will teach you how to play notes on the beat using the two different time signatures. Place your violin and bow in playing position, and set your 1st finger B on the A string. In compound time, set your metronome to 40, and change to a new bow stroke on each of the four clicks of the metronome. In simple time, set your metronome to 60, and change to a new bow stroke on each of the four clicks of the metronome. Repeat the measures as needed (see Figure 4.60).

- *Divisions of Beat*—This exercise will teach you how to play smaller divisions of the beat using the two different time signatures. Place your violin and bow in playing position, and set your 1st finger B on the A string. In compound time, set your metronome to 40, play three separate short bow strokes within the first click of the metronome, and play six very short and quick bow strokes within the second beat. In simple time, set your metronome to 60, and play two short bow strokes within the first click of the metronome, two short bow strokes within the second click of the metronome, four very short and quick bow strokes within the third click of the metronome, and four very short and quick bow strokes within the fourth click of the metronome. Repeat the measures as needed (see Figure 4.61).

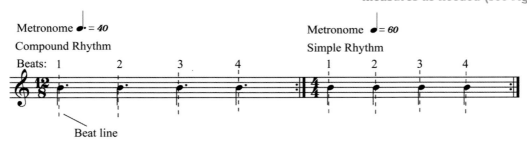

Figure 4.60
Beat Notes rhythm exercise

Figure 4.61
Divisions of Beat rhythm exercise

🎶 *Holding Beats*—This exercise will teach you how to play longer rhythms of the beat using the two different time signatures. Place your violin and bow in playing position and set your 1st finger B on the A string. In compound time, set your metronome to 40, sustain a single bow stroke over the first and second clicks of the metronome, and sustain another single bow stroke over the third and fourth clicks of the metronome. In simple time, set your metronome to 60 and sustain a single bow stroke over all four clicks of the metronome. Repeat the measures as needed (see Figure 4.62).

🎶 *Dotted Rhythms*—This exercise will teach you how to play dotted rhythms of the beat using the two different time signatures. Place your violin and bow in playing position and set your 1st finger B on the A string. In compound time, set your metronome to 40, play a single bow stroke within the first click of the metronome, and then play three separate short bow strokes within the second click of the metronome. In simple time, set your metronome to 60, and in the second measure, sustain a single bow stroke over the first three clicks of the metronome, and then play another note on the fourth click of the metronome. In the third measure, sustain a single bow stroke over the first and second clicks of the metronome, stop the bow just after the second click to prepare to play a short bow stroke between beats two and three, then sustain a single bow stroke over the third and fourth clicks of the metronome, and stop the bow just after the fourth click to prepare to play a short bow stroke between beats four and one of the new measure. In measure four, start a bow stroke on the first click and play a short bow stroke just before the second click, start a new bow stroke on the second click and play a short bow stroke just before the third click, start another new bow stroke on the third click and play a short bow stroke just before the fourth click, and start a bow stroke on the fourth click and play a short bow stroke just before the first click of a new measure. Repeat the measures as needed (see Figure 4.63 on next page).

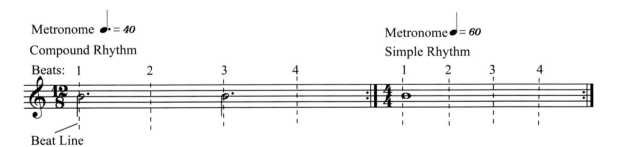

Figure 4.62
Holding Beats rhythm exercise

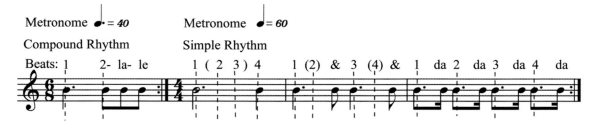

Figure 4.63
Dotted Rhythm exercise

🎵 *Mixtures*—This exercise will transition you into a rhythmic expert by using the two different time signatures. Place your violin and bow in playing position and set your 1st finger B on the A string. In compound time, set your metronome to 40, play a single bow stroke within the first click of the metronome, play three separate short bow strokes within the second click, play another bow stroke on the third click of the metronome. and then play another short bow stroke just before the first click of the new measure. In simple time, set your metronome to 60, and in the second measure play a single bow stroke on the first click, play two short bow strokes within the second click, play a long bow stroke sustaining over the third and fourth clicks, and stop the bow just after the fourth click to prepare to play another bow stroke between the fourth and first click of the new measure. In the third measure, play a single bow stroke sustaining over the first and second clicks of the metronome, play a bow stroke on the third click and then a second short bow stroke just before the fourth click of the metronome, and then play four very short and quick bow strokes within the fourth click of the metronome. Repeat the measures as needed (see Figure 4.64).

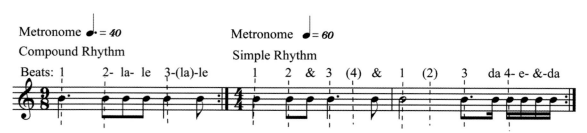

Figure 4.64
Mixtures rhythm exercise

88

Rhythmic Specialties

In music, there are a few symbols that can alter rhythm or override the set tempo. These symbols can give the musician total control on how much to alter a rhythm, or they can have a set perimeter with a marked tempo that the musician must ultimately reach.

Here are a few rhythmic specialties that can alter rhythm:

- *Accelerando, accel.*—To gradually make the tempo faster.

- *Ritardando, rit.*—To gradually make the tempo slower.

- *A Tempo*—Usually written after a ritardando, meaning to return to the original tempo.

- *Fermata*—The ability to hold a note longer than its rhythmic value (see Figure 4.65).

- *Triplet*—To allow a grouping of three notes to replace the rhythmic timing of two notes (see Figure 4.66).

Figure 4.65
Fermata

Figure 4.66
Triplet

Specialty

Techniques

PICTURE YOURSELF DAZZLING YOUR audience with specialty sound effects that leap off your violin with exciting percussive bow strokes, gorgeous vibrato, and flying fingers. This chapter will teach you step-by-step how to place your bow, how much speed and pressure to use, and how to move your fingers to achieve a wonderful mastery of violin techniques.

Specialty Fingerings

I N MUSIC, A VIOLINIST NEEDS to be able to read and interpret certain specialty fingering techniques that will add to the ambiance of a performance. These specialty-fingering techniques can simply highlight a particular note, or fill each note with warmth, color, and emotion.

Ornamentation

Ornamentation adds musical flourishes to a melodic phrase by decorating or "ornamenting" a certain main note. A composer can ornament a main note by simply adding one smaller note to it, or by highlighting the main note with many surrounding smaller notes.

Grace Note

An ornamenting *grace note* is a small note that precedes a normal rhythmic note. In music, there can be a single grace note or there can be many grace notes, depending on the effect the composer wanted to create. To perform a grace note, simply start the slur on the tiny grace note and quickly slur in the normal written note, in a "short-long" rhythm (see the DVD).

Here are the two ways a grace note can affect rhythm:

❦ *The subtracting grace note*—The grace note is in the same measure as the normal attached note. Both notes will share the same original rhythmic beat as a "short-long" rhythm (see Figure 5.1).

Figure 5.1
Subtracting grace note

❦ *The anticipating grace note*—The grace note is separated from the normal attached note by a measure bar line. In performance, you play a clearly heard grace note and then play the normal attached note for its full rhythmic beat (see Figure 5.2).

Figure 5.2
Anticipating grace note

Trill

In music, the ornamenting *tr.* sign is written over a note that is meant to be performed as a trill. A trill is when you hold the written note down on the string with pressure and repetitively tap the next pitch higher onto the same string, according to the key signature, in a single slur.

Written Note

When performing ornamentations, you must always start and end on the written note. For example, if a B is written in the music with ornamentation, you will start with the B, do the ornamentation, and then end with the B.

Here's how to perform a trill (see Figure 5.3 and the DVD):

Figure 5.3
1st finger B trill

1. Begin the slur with your 1st finger B, on the A string.

2. Continue the slur while you tap-tap-tap your Low 2 C♮ on the red tape.

3. End the slur with your 1st finger B, on the A string.

Key Signature

You must trill according to the key signature. If you have a C♯ in the key signature, and you are trilling on a B, you need to tap-tap-tap a High 2 on the gold tape C♯ (see Figure 5.4).

Figure 5.4
1st finger B trilling to a C♯

Mordent

In music, this ornamentation is noted by a ∾ sign above a normal note or simply written out by grace notes after a normal note. The mordent will share the original rhythmic beat with the normal attached note, and as always, you need to start and end with the written pitch.

Here's how to perform the mordent (see Figure 5.5 and the DVD):

Figure 5.5
Mordent on C

> "Playing the violin comes down to that one magical, unforgettable moment, when you are trembling on stage, lights piecing your eyes, and you are drenched in sweat with nervous thoughts racing through your head. You begin playing, and the moment the first note sings itself out of your violin, the faces of the audience are no longer visible. Then the music sweeps you into a magical universe where you have never been, yet it is familiar to you, like you have lived there all your life, and you realize, it is not about the audience, it is about you. As you play, the music bubbles up from your heart and soul, and suddenly, you and the violin are one. A shining star where the light comes straight from the passion of your performance, and with every note, more light sings itself from the depths of your soul, and you fill the world with light from your sheer joy beyond anything you've ever experienced. All the misery and sorrow in your life no longer exists, for the music has transformed itself into true happiness within you. Then, without warning, the audience bursts into wild applause because they felt it too—the light and pure joy you were radiating. Because in the end, when music comes from your heart, not your fingers, you will know you have truly become a violinist. I know that a person does not have to be gifted or be a prodigy to play the violin. All you need is a little heart and soul mixed with the desire to share your joy with the world."
>
> —Serene, 13 years old

1. Begin a slur on the long original written note, Low 2 red tape C, on the A string.

2. Slur in a short note above the written note, 3rd finger D.

3. Slur in a short original written note, Low 2 C.

4. Slur in a short note below the written note, 1st finger B.

5. End the slur on the original written note, Low 2 red tape C.

Fingers Touching

The *mordent* is performed with a minor second below the written note, or a half step (fingers touching). If you had to perform a mordent on the written note 3rd finger D and the key signature did not have a C♯, you would have to add a sharp to the mordent (∾) in order to create the minor second below the D, thus making the 3rd finger D and High 2 finger C♯ on the gold tape touch to create a half step (see Figure 5.6).

Figure 5.6
Mordent on D

Fingering Signs

Many different fingering signs can appear above certain notes in music that require special fingering techniques with your left fingering hand. These techniques can add a different color or mood to a performance, as well as provide a textured sound effect.

Harmonics

A harmonic is noted by a small "o" sign above certain notes. To perform a harmonic, only one finger should lightly touch the string in the center of a harmonic location and the bow should move quickly near the bridge. This technique will create a whistle sound effect, and when bowed properly, should ring fairly loudly.

There are many natural harmonic locations on the string, but the truest of all natural harmonics are the octaves above the open strings (see Figure 5.7). The location of the octave harmonic is exactly half the distance of the string between the nut and the bridge (see Figure 5.8). The other harmonics are at every halfway point on the string from above and below the octave harmonic.

A false harmonic is noted by a small clear diamond-shaped note head directly above a normal note head on the staff (see Figure 5.9). To generate a false harmonic sound, press your 1st finger down on the string and lightly touch your 4th finger on the same string (see Figure 5.10). A violinist can create a false harmonic on any point of the string by shifting the entire hand and thumb up the neck of the violin while keeping the 1st and 4th fingers locked in the same position and moving from tape to tape (see the DVD).

Figure 5.7
The octave harmonic

Figure 5.8
4th finger creating the octave harmonic

Figure 5.9
The false harmonic

Figure 5.10
Creating a false harmonic

Left Pizzicato

A left-handed pizzicato is noted by a small + sign above any note (see Figure 5.11). This symbol tells a violinist to pluck the string using the left fingering hand. The note with the + sign above needs to be the sounding note, and you can use any of the upper fingers to pluck the string.

Figure 5.11
Open string left pizzicato

Fingered Left-Handed Pizzicato

Hold the fingered note that has the + sign, with pressure on the string. Offset an upper finger to the left side of the string onto the fingerboard. Heavily drag the tip of the upper finger over the desired string, while slightly lifting/gripping the string with the pad of the left finger, to create a plucking sound (see Figure 5.12).

Figure 5.12
Fingered note left pizzicato

Extensions

A finger extension is noted by an *ext.* or ⌢, in music (see Figure 5.13). This fingering technique is highly useful when a note is just out of the 1st–4th finger range and you do not want to shift into another position or change to a higher string. For example, if you are on the A string, playing 4th finger E, and the next note is one pitch higher, F♮, you can simply extend your 4th finger just above the 4th finger tape on the A string to create an F♮ pitch instead of having to release all four fingers, change strings with your bow, and pull back your hand for a Low 1 on the E string (see the DVD).

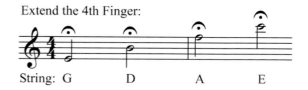

Figure 5.13
4th finger extension

Glissando

A *glissando* is a fingering technique that creates a sliding sound effect that glides along each chromatic step (or every flat, natural, and sharp for each note) from one written note to the next written note. It can be performed with any finger, and sometimes it can be performed with a certain chromatic combination of fingers. A violinist needs to learn how to glissando moving up and down the string.

Here are the various types of glissandos:

- *Half-step chromatic glissando* (see Figure 5.14)—Sliding any finger up or down from its Low position to its High position. Low 1 to Regular 1 on the tape, Low 2 to High 2, Regular 3 to High 3, Regular 4 to an Extension 4 (see the DVD).

- *Glissando shift* (see Figure 5.15)—Sliding your entire hand to a new position by gliding on any one finger from one tape to another tape. For example, to perform a glissando shift from your 1st finger tape, you slide your hand and thumb up the violin neck and fingerboard by simply closing your left elbow, until your 1st finger reaches any other tape on the same string. Let your 1st finger glide along the string with slight pressure while you slur with the bow from one tape to another tape to create a sliding sound effect (see the DVD).

- *Harmonic glissando* (see Figure 5.16)—Slide your entire hand to a harmonic, like a glissando shift, but you glide along the string without pressure and you add a downward scooping action into the string with the finger as you near the harmonic location. For example, start with your 4th finger on the 4th finger tape and glide your 4th finger along the string by lightly touching the

Figure 5.14
Half-step chromatic glissando

Figure 5.15
Glissando shift

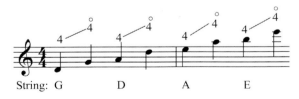

Figure 5.16
Harmonic glissando

string until you come near to the harmonic octave location, then dip the finger into the string with pressure as you scoop and then release the string pressure sliding right into the harmonic octave. The bow can either lift off the string at the exact moment you arrive at the harmonic octave, thus creating a ringing sound effect, or it can continue bowing a longer bow stroke, making the harmonic tone lengthen in rhythmic time (see the DVD).

Fingering Combinations

A violinist is required to use fingering combinations to achieve different musical sound effects. These fingering combinations can provide the violinist with an easy, systematic way to cleanly perform a technically demanding series of chromatic notes.

Chromatic Fingering

A *chromatic fingering* is a certain combination of fingers that creates a chromatic glissando effect over a wide range of notes, covering an entire string or multiple strings. This particular fingering combination allows the violinist to play a separate finger for each stepwise chromatic note, giving clarity to each note, eliminating the sliding sound effect when chromatic notes share the same sliding finger. To perform the chromatic fingering in Figure 5.17, place your bow on the A string and play an open A, then Low 1 B♭. Set your 2nd finger on the 1st gold tape touching your Low 1, scoot your 1st finger up to your Low 2 red tape, and set your 2nd finger on the High 2 gold tape. Set your 3rd finger on the 3rd tape and set your 4th finger between the 3rd and 4th gold tapes. Then, release all fingers as you roll your bow to the open E string.

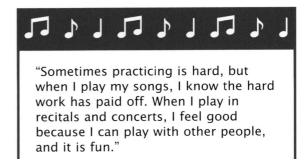

"Sometimes practicing is hard, but when I play my songs, I know the hard work has paid off. When I play in recitals and concerts, I feel good because I can play with other people, and it is fun."

—Jackson, 7 years old

Figure 5.17
Chromatic fingering

Double Stops

A *double stop* is when a violinist performs two notes simultaneously on the violin. A double stop can be any combination of fingers and can even be slurred to other single notes or double stops. When bowing a double stop, simply balance the natural weight of the bow equally on both strings, and gently draw the equally balanced bow across the strings without adding any extra pressure from the bow.

There are two types of double stops:

- ❧ *Double stops with opens* (see Figure 5.18) —An open string with another open string, or an open string with a fingered string (see the DVD).

- ❧ *Fingered double stops* (see Figure 5.19)— Both strings are fingered by the same or different finger.

Figure 5.18
Double stops with opens

Slur Articulation

It is necessary to strike your fingers onto the string to form rhythmic articulation to each note in a smooth slur. It is easy to have rhythmic clarity when you perform separate bows, because the changing of bowing direction from down bow to up bow automatically articulates the start of each note. In contrast, a slur is unable to use the changing of bow direction to add articulation to each separate note, and must rely on striking the fingers onto the string to clean up a muddled or sloppy sounding tone. This technique is done on a slur with ascending notes so that the next finger higher can strike the string forcibly to achieve rhythmic clarity and articulation to the start of each note (see Figure 5.20).

Figure 5.19
Fingered double stops

Figure 5.20
Ascending slur

Vibrato

Many musicians believe that the violinist's vibrato can breathe life into a note, inspiring its shape, purpose, meaning, and above all, emotional value. Vibrato can take many months or even years to master, but the following four-step method can get you started on the fast track.

Here's the four-step method to learn vibrato (see the DVD):

1. *Palm line slide* (see Figure 5.21): With your violin in playing position and no bow, set your thumb and palm line in the fingering position. Slightly remove the palm line from the side of the fingerboard, creating a gap of air. Open and close your left elbow to make your palm line glide along the side of the fingerboard from 1st fingering tape to the Low 1 position, while you use your thumb as an anchor to center your hand around 1st tape.

2. *Finger rock*: Set your 3rd finger on the 3rd tape and continue to slide your palm line without pressure along the side of the fingerboard. Keep the tip of the finger directly centered on the 3rd tape, and let your finger knuckles arch up (see Figure 5.22) and straighten back (see Figure 5.23) as your elbow moves your palm line. This motion will roll your finger tip along the string, which causes the pitch to rise to a sharp pitch and lower to a flat pitch, creating the vibrato effect. Repeat this step using each separate finger.

3. *Pepperoni sounds*: Create a long smooth slur using the entire length of your bow, while you rock your finger slowly up and down two times using the palm line slide. The sound effect sounds like "pep-per-ro-ni" down bow, and "pep-per-ro-ni" up bow. Repeat this step on each separate finger.

4. *Counting vibrato hits*: Each time you bring your hand near the shoulder of the violin, pretend that the side of your hand hits the violin, creating a steady back-and-forth hand motion through the elbow and relaxed wrist. Try to increase the number of vibrato hits on a single bow stroke until you reach eight steady vibrato hits down bow and then up bow.

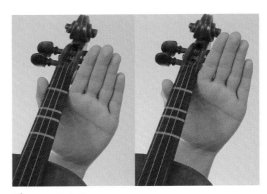

Figure 5.21
Palm line slide

Figure 5.22
Finger rock
arch-up

Figure 5.23
Finger rock
straighten-back

Specialty Bowings

THE BOW IS THE SOUNDING voice of the violin, and it can create many unique sound effects. Take your time in discovering the different character tones for each of the following bow strokes. A violinist is required to perfect each bowing's sound effect, and to be able to change from one bow stroke to another effortlessly.

Smooth Strokes

Creating a smooth tone builds a foundation for all other sound effects, because it teaches you to control your bowing technique and to develop a perceptive ear to achieve a flawless tone quality.

Legato

A *legato* bow stroke creates a normal, smooth, connected tone without any special sound effects (see the DVD). The legato bow stroke can use any length of bow, can be performed on any part of the bow, and can also have any volume, or *dynamic*, from soft to loud. When performing a legato slur, move the bow in a smooth continuous bow stroke, connecting all the notes under the slur together. If the music calls for two of the same notes to be legato slurred together, notice that the two same notes will be combined into one long slurred note (see Figure 5.24).

Detache

A *detache* bow stroke simply means a detached note. The shaping of a detache bow stroke has a slight increase in pressure near the middle of the bow stroke, creating a gentle swell in volume or dynamic followed by a release of pressure at the end of the bow stroke, which results in a decrease in volume. If the music calls for two or more notes to be detache slurred together, you will gently swell the center of each note with speed and pressure before gently stopping between each note, to create two separate notes in the same bow direction (see Figure 5.25).

Here's how to perform a detache bow stroke (see the DVD):

1. Begin the bow stroke near the upper half of the bow with little speed and pressure of the bow.

2. As you approach the center of the note, gently increase the speed and lean into the index finger of your bow hold to increase the pressure of the bow on the string.

3. To end the note, release the pressure of the index finger and decrease the speed of the bow to relax the sound.

4. Come to a gentle stop before creating the next detache bow stroke.

Figure 5.24
Legato notes

Figure 5.25
Detache notes

Short Strokes

Rhythm is divided into two basic forms: long notes and short notes. The short notes can be performed in different variations of texture and ringing quality, depending on the bowing technique applied to the string.

Figure 5.26
Square zone

Scrub

The *scrub* bow stroke is performed near the middle of the bow, in the *square zone,* where your bow, violin, upper arm, and lower arm form the four sides of a square shape (see Figure 5.26). This location of the bow combined with the arm shape generates the most powerful, articulate, and clean sound from the bow with a minimal amount of body effort by simply leaning into the index finger of your bow hold to apply heavy pressure onto the string (see the DVD). The tiny motions of your elbow, wrist, and the side-to-side bow hand exercises will work together to form repeated short, scrubby notes on the string, near the middle of the bow (see Figure 5.27).

Figure 5.27
Scrub notes

Staccato

The *staccato* bow stroke is very similar to the scrub bow stroke, but with the distinction of a definite stop of the bow on the string to separate each staccato note. The stop is created by quickly stopping the bow on the string with pressure from your index finger and thumb of your bow hold (see the DVD). If the music calls for two or more notes to be staccato slurred together, you will stop and re-articulate the bow before each note to create two distinctively separated notes in the same bow direction (see Figure 5.28).

Spiccato

The *spiccato* bow stroke is a horizontally dropped brush stroke that will bounce on and off the string. To control the bouncing effect on and off the string, you incorporate techniques of the claw up-and-down bow hold finger exercises with the side-to-side bow hold finger exercises, as you change bow directions through the cross over bow arm movement.

Here's how to perform a spiccato bow stroke (see the DVD):

1. Hover the bow just above the string near the frog of the bow.

2. Slowly begin to "air bow" the string, by beginning a small downward bow stroke with the cross over bow arm movement.

3. Gradually drop the bow onto the string.

4. Let about an inch of bow dip down into the string by using the bow hold finger exercise techniques, brushing the bow hairs and string together.

5. Lift the bow off the string with the continued cross over bow arm movement to create a ringing effect before creating the next upward spiccato bow stroke.

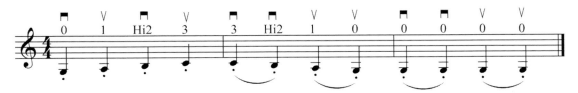

Figure 5.28
Staccato notes

Bow Placement

A *staccato* can be performed at any location on the bow for different textures and volume levels, but the most common location is the square zone for a medium/loud tone.

Bow Placement

A repeated fast spiccato is performed just above the square zone, allowing the vibrations of the bow to self-perpetuate the spiccato bounce, whereas a slower, more controlled spiccato is performed at the frog of the bow, allowing the cross over bow arm movement to control a slower-paced bounce (see Figure 5.29).

Figure 5.29
Spiccato notes

Commanding Strokes

A commanding performance is another character sound effect that a violinist must practice to perfection. A great violinist has charisma and confidence on stage, with the knowledge of the exact scientific method of bow placement, pressure, and speed that can create a power note.

Accents

An *accent* affects only the initial starting tone of a bow stroke, and the rest of an accented bow sounds like a normal legato bow stroke of any length and dynamic. The accent is formed by pinching your bow with the index finger and thumb of the bow hold, thus causing the bow to grip the string (see Figure 5.30). In music, an accent sign can be placed above any value of note with any level of volume or dynamic (see Figure 5.31).

Figure 5.30
Bow hold pinch

Here's how to perform an accented bow stroke (see the DVD):

1. Press down on your bow with your index finger and thumb, causing the bow to lean into the string, forming a gripping sensation.

2. As you perform the bow stroke with a quick speed, you will notice a pop or an accent to the start of the note from the bow hold pinch.

3. Relax the lean of your index finger and reduce speed to create a release of pressure to the note.

4. Perform the remainder of the note with a normal legato bow stroke.

Figure 5.31
Accent notes

Resets

A *reset* is performed between two down bows in a row that are not marked by a slur (see Figure 5.32). To get from one down bow to the other, simply lift your bow off the string after the first down bow stroke, and reset it near the frog of your bow to begin the second down bow. Resets are generally performed at the lower half near the frog of the bow because the bow hairs are firmer and will reduce the amount of uncontrollable bounce when you "reset" the bow onto the string (see the DVD).

Up-Bow Lifts

An *up-bow lift* is when you lift the bow off the string between an up bow and a down bow to create a ringing tone that resonates in the air. In performance, you want to stay in the lower half, hitting the down bow on the string at the frog of the bow to create a loud and forceful sound at the beginning of the down bow stroke (see Figure 5.33).

Here's how to perform an up-bow lift (see the DVD):

1. Perform the up bow with a quick push off and lift near the lower half of the bow, to create a ringing tone that resonates in the air.

2. While in mid-air, keep the arm's momentum moving toward the frog and change bow direction to a down bow.

3. Hit the bow hair on the string to form a pop or a down-bow accent, reducing the speed of the bow to transition the down bow into a normal legato tone.

Figure 5.32
Reset down bows

Figure 5.33
Up-bow lifts

Martale

A *martale* bow stroke is the fastest and the loudest bow stroke in a violinist's repertoire. It is performed in the upper half near the tip of the bow, and you combine a sudden whip-like start with a heavy pinch of the bow with a detache ending (see Figure 5.34).

Martale Resets

A violinist can also perform fast multiple down bow resets with a martale sound by hitting each reset hard on the string at the frog of the bow (see Figure 5.35).

Here's how to perform a martale bow stroke (see the DVD):

1. Place your bow on the string near the bridge, between the upper half and the tip of the bow.

2. Pinch the bow by using your index finger and thumb to lean the bow hard into the string.

3. With a sudden whip-like motion, jerk your elbow open with extreme speed as you release the bow hold pinch.

4. In the last two inches of the bow, slow the bow speed and transition the stroke into a light detache ending.

5. Stop the bow completely and re-grip the string with a bow hold pinch before creating the next martale bow stroke.

Figure 5.34
Martale notes

Figure 5.35
Martale resets

Bowing Sound Effects

Sometimes a violinist needs to think outside of a beautiful warm vibrato and proper finger accuracy when learning to achieve a specialty sound effect with the bow. The main focus is the sound effect the bow is creating, and whether it can be understood by the audience.

Collegno

A *collegno* bow stroke is a special sound effect of bouncing the wood of the bow, several times in a down bow slur, on a string (see Figure 5.36). This sound effect gives an eerie tone to the music for a muted percussive character tone. The first occurring sound is the controlled drop of the bow, whereas the following notes bounce along the wood of the bow in a natural, self-perpetuating, bouncing pattern (see Figure 5.37).

Figure 5.36
Collegno bow stroke

Here's how to perform a collegno bow stroke (see the DVD):

1. Flip the bow upside down, or tilt the bow away from you, until only the wood of the bow touches the string.

2. Hover the bow over the string within the lower half of the bow.

3. Begin to "air bow" a downwards stroke as you gradually drop the wood of the bow into the string.

4. Let the bow bounce off the string several times while pulling a slow down bow slur with a medium pressure from your bow hold index finger.

5. Stop the bow on the string, reset to the lower half of the bow, and perform another collegno bow stroke.

Figure 5.37
Collegno notes

Ricochet

A *ricochet* bow stroke is very similar to a collegno bow stroke in performance, but the ricochet is performed by using the hair of the bow, which will naturally grip the string, requiring a more perceptive ear to achieve a precise and clean tone (see Figure 5.38).

Here's how to perform a ricochet bow stroke (see the DVD):

1. Hover the bow hairs over the string within the lower half of the bow.

2. Begin to "air bow" a downward stroke as you vertically drop (or *hatchet*) the bow into the string. The vertical drop will cause the bow to bounce off the string higher, perpetuating the motion for the remainder of the bounces to come in the same slurred down bow.

3. Let the bow horizontally bounce off the string several times while pulling a slow down bow slur with a medium pressure from your bow hold index finger.

4. Stop the bow on the string, reset to the lower half of the bow, and perform another ricochet bow stroke, or give a tiny yet forceful single up bow stroke to the end your ricochet bow.

Tremolo

A *tremolo* bow stroke is a succession of short, fast strokes near the tip of the bow (see the DVD). A violinist needs to perform as many short up-and-down bow strokes as possible into a tremolo note, by repeatedly flexing the elbow in tiny, quick, oscillating motions while leaning into the index finger of the bow hold (see Figure 5.39).

Figure 5.38
Ricochet notes

Figure 5.39
Tremolo notes

Musical Phrasing

MUSICAL PHRASING IS THE LAST step in learning how to express emotion, color, and excitement to your audience. Think of musical phrasing as a roller coaster of emotions with suspense, twists and turns, expected and unexpected dips, climaxes, and happy or tragic endings.

Dynamics

Dynamics refers to a range in volume from soft to loud, performed in music. To achieve this range in volume and reach any dynamic goal, a violinist must consider a combination of the five main factors of speed, pressure, string placement, bow placement, and vibrato.

Here's how to correctly achieve the main levels of musical dynamics:

- *PP or Pianissimo, very soft*—Slow speed, no pressure, over the fingerboard, tip of the bow, and no vibrato.

- *P or Piano, soft*—Slow speed, slight pressure, near the fingerboard, tip of the bow, and no vibrato.

- *MP or Mezzo-Piano, medium soft*—Medium speed, light pressure, center of the string, upper half of the bow, slow vibrato.

- *MF or Mezzo-Forte, medium loud*—Medium speed, medium pressure, center of the string, middle of the bow, medium vibrato.

- *F or Forte, loud*—Fast speed, heavy pressure, center of the string, lower half of the bow, fast vibrato.

- *FF or Fortissimo, very loud*—Fast speed, forceful pressure, near to the bridge, frog of the bow, fast and wide vibrato.

Special Effects with Dynamics

Now that you know how to scientifically achieve each level of technical sound effects with the fingers and bow, it is time to start mixing them together to master your new craft.

Crescendo

A *crescendo* means to get louder through dynamics over time (see Figure 5.40). Typically, you will start at Piano and increase your speed, pressure, and vibrato while you move the bow closer to the frog and near the bridge until you reach a louder tone. To achieve a crescendo slur over a number of beats, you need to think about bow proportions, or the amount of bow length for each beat.

Figure 5.40
Crescendo

Here's how to proportion your bow over a four-beat crescendo:

1. The first beat will be Piano and will only need about an inch of bow with little pressure.

2. The second beat will be Mezzo-Piano and will only need two inches of bow with little pressure.

3. The third beat will be Mezzo-Forte and will need up to the middle of the bow with medium pressure.

4. The fourth beat will be Forte and will use the entire length of the second half of the bow with heavy pressure.

Here's how to proportion your bow over a four-beat decrescendo:

1. The first beat will be Forte and will use the entire length of the first half of the bow with heavy pressure.

2. The second beat will be Mezzo-Forte and will need up to the middle of the second half of the bow with medium pressure.

3. The third beat will be Mezzo-Piano and will need only two inches of bow with little pressure.

4. The fourth beat will be Piano and will need only about an inch of bow with little pressure.

Decrescendo

Decrescendo (also called *diminuendo*) means to get softer through dynamics over time. Typically you will start at Forte and reduce your speed, pressure, and vibrato while you move the bow closer to the tip and near the fingerboard until you reach a softer tone. To achieve a decrescendo slur over a number of beats you need to think about bow proportions, or the amount of bow length for each beat (see Figure 5.41).

Figure 5.41
Decrescendo

Sudden Bursts of Tone

There are two main bowing techniques to perform a sudden burst of tone: a Sforzando (sF) and a forzando (Fz). These musical symbols describe both a dynamic change and a bowing articulation to be performed by a violinist. In performance, both of the musical symbols will feel like a giant martale, but with a sudden burst of vibrato speed at the start of the note, called a *stinger vibrato*. To create a stinger vibrato, suddenly start a fast and aggressive vibrato with the initial pull of the bow to form a short burst of ringing tone.

- *sF, Sforzando* (see Figure 5.42)—Formed by a heavy bow hold pinch with a quick starting speed of the bow, near the bridge, combined with a stinger vibrato. The dynamic will remain Forte.

- *Fz, Forzando* (see Figure 5.43)—Formed by a heavy bow hold pinch with a quick starting speed of the bow, near the bridge, combined with a stinger vibrato. The dynamic will decrescendo to Piano.

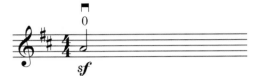

Figure 5.42
sF note

Figure 5.43
Fz note

Beginner
Songs

PICTURE YOURSELF PLAYING YOUR FIRST song on the violin while reading from sheet music written for a violinist. In this chapter, you will combine all learned knowledge from the previous chapters and be able to count rhythms, read note names, understand the key signature, and follow the bowings with the help from a measure-by-measure guide that will show you how to set each finger and bow for every note. This easy-to-follow, measure-by-measure guide will walk you through your first songs and help you successfully navigate through each musical phrase. Once you feel confident on reading the sheet music, you can replay the songs over and over again using just the sheet music provided for each song, and if you find that you need a little extra help with a particular note, the measure-by-measure guide will be right there to give you the tools you need to perform each song with confidence.

Practicing Techniques

GOOD PRACTICE TECHNIQUES are composed of how much time you should practice everyday, how to warm up, and how to learn your song. Ideally, you should practice at least 15-20 minutes every day, on up to 30 minutes for beginners, 45-60 minutes for intermediates, and 1-2 hours for advance players in high school. Music majors in college and violin professionals can easily spend over eight hours everyday with their instrument in hand. The length of practice time should equal the amount of time it takes you to tune, warm up on finger patterns or scales, and practice your song. As you progress, more and more technique books can be added to your daily routine and the violin solos eventually will become longer and longer, which can lengthen your practice time.

Once you have tuned the violin and have warmed up on the finger pattern or scale that directly relates to your song, it is time to practice. I recommend the following five-step method to learning any new song:

1. Read all note names out loud in relation to the key signature.

2. Cover the rhythm by clapping with the metronome and singing the long and short rhythms in each measure.

3. Learn measure (mm.) 1 by reviewing the note names, double-checking the High and Low fingers, saying the rhythm with the metronome, and playing the measure over and over again with the bow until it feels comfortable.

4. Learn the next measure, by reviewing the note names, double-checking the High and Low fingers, saying the rhythm with the metronome, and playing the measure over and over again with the bow until it feels comfortable. Then play all learned measures together until they fit comfortably with the metronome. Repeat this step until all measures are learned.

5. Focus on the notes you had trouble getting the first time in a measure by practicing them slowly at first and then smoothly speeding it up to tempo, or the suggested metronome marking. As you approach a hard section when playing a song, think about how to successfully navigate through the difficult notes so that it will not catch you by surprise.

"Playing the violin is like solving a math problem. When it's too easy, one becomes bored. When it's too hard, one feels overwhelmed. However, when it is just challenging enough, and you accomplish it, one feels satisfied."

—Mengxiang, 16 years old

Ba Ba Black Sheep

Basic song characteristics:

- Metronome: Quarter note = 60.

- Key signature: A Major, three sharps: F ♯, C ♯, and G ♯.

- Time signature: Simple, four beats per measure, and the quarter note gets the beat. Half note = 2 beats, quarter note = 1 beat, eighth note = $\frac{1}{2}$ beat.

- Strings: A string = High 2 finger pattern, E string = High 2 finger pattern.

- Note names, first line: A, A, E, E // F ♯, F ♯, F ♯, F ♯, E // D, D, C ♯, C ♯ // B, B, A// (the // represents a bar line between measures).

- Rhythm, first line: Long-long-long-long // short-short-short-short-very long // long-long-long-long // long-long-very long//.

- Technical difficulty: Going from the Open E string to 3rd finger D, by quickly moving the bow to the A string and setting down your 1, High 2, and 3 (measures 3, 5, 7, and 11).

- See the DVD for a performance of the song with the metronome.

Here's how to play the song measure by measure:

mm1. Place your bow on the A string near the lower half and play two long Open A's, starting down bow, stop and roll over to the E string and play two long Open E's, starting down bow.

mm2. Set your 1st finger on the E string, and play four short F ♯'s at the lower half of the bow. Remove your 1st finger and play a very long Open E string, the full length of the down bow.

mm3. Roll over to the A string and set your 1, High 2, and 3rd finger D. Play two long D's, starting up bow, and remove your 3rd finger to play two long C ♯'s, starting up bow.

mm4. Continue the musical phrase and remove your 2nd finger to play two long B's, up bow. Remove your 1st finger and play a very long Open A, the full length of your up bow.

mm5. Roll over to the Open E string and play a long down bow, followed by two short E's at the tip of your bow. Roll back to the A string and set your 1, High 2, and 3rd finger D. Play two long D's, starting up bow.

mm6. Continue the musical phrase by removing your 3rd finger to play a long C ♯ followed by two short C ♯'s at the frog of the bow. Remove your 2nd finger to play a very long 1st finger B, down bow.

mm7. Roll over to the Open E string and play a long up bow, followed by two short E's at the frog of the bow. Roll back to the A string and set your 1, High 2, and 3rd finger D. Play four short D's at the frog of the bow.

mm8. Continue the musical phrase by removing your 3rd finger to play a long C♯ followed by two short C♯'s at the tip of the bow. Remove your 2nd finger to play a very long 1st finger B, the full length of the up bow.

mm9. Place your bow on the A string and play two long Open A's, starting down bow; stop and roll over to the E string and play two long Open E's, starting down bow.

mm10. Set your 1st finger on the E string, and play four short F♯'s at the frog of the bow. Remove your 1st finger and play a very long Open E string the full length of the down bow.

mm11. Roll over to the A string and set your 1, High 2, and 3rd finger D. Play two long D's, starting up bow, and remove your 3rd finger to play two long C♯'s, starting up bow.

mm12. Continue the musical phrase and remove your 2nd finger to play two long B's, up bow. Remove your 1st finger and play a very long Open A, the full length of the up bow.

Folk Song

Figure 7.1
Ba Ba Black Sheep

Lightly Row

Basic song characteristics:

- Metronome: Quarter note = 72.

- Key signature: A Major, three sharps: F♯, C♯, and G♯.

- Time signature: Simple, four beats per measure, and the quarter note gets the beat. Half note = 2 beats, quarter note = 1 beat.

- Strings: A string = High 2 finger pattern, E string = High 2 finger pattern.

- Note names, first line: E, C♯, C♯ // D, B, B // A, B, C♯, D // E, E, E//.

- Rhythm, first line: Long-long-very long // long-long-very long // long-long-long-long // long-long-very long//.

- Fingering technical difficulty: Setting the High 2 C♯ on the A string without setting another finger with the High 2 C♯ (measures 7, 8, 15, and 16). Setting the High 2 C♯ and at the same time setting the 1st finger B, while preparing to set the 3rd finger D (measures 1, 2, 5, 6, 13, and 14).

- See the DVD for a performance of the song with the metronome.

Here's how to play the song measure by measure:

mm1. Hover your 2nd finger over the High 2 tape on the A string. Place your bow near the lower half on the Open E string and play a long Open E, down bow. Roll over to the A string, set down your High 2 C♯ and play a long up bow, followed by another C♯ with a very long down bow using the full length of the bow.

mm2. Hold your High 2 and set down your 1st and 3rd finger on the A string. Play a long up bow on 3rd finger D, and then remove your 3rd and 2nd finger to play 1st finger B with a long down bow, followed by another 1st finger B with a very long up bow, using the full length of the bow.

mm3. Remove your 1st finger and play a High 2 finger pattern on the Open A string, starting down bow, play Open A, then 1st finger, High 2, and 3rd finger. Each note will get a separate long bow.

mm4. Roll over to the Open E string and play two long E's, starting down bow, followed by a very long E using the full length of the down bow.

mm5. Play a long Open E, up bow. Roll over to the A string, set down your 1st finger and High 2 C♯, and play three long C♯'s, starting down bow.

mm6. Hold your 1st finger and High 2 while you set down your 3rd finger on the A string. Play a long up bow on 3rd finger D, and then remove your 3rd and 2nd finger to play 1st finger B with three long bows, starting down bow.

mm7. Remove your 1st finger and play an Open A with a long up bow. Set your High 2 C♯ and play a long down bow. Roll over to the Open E string as you remove your High 2, and play Open E with two long bows, starting up bow.

mm8. Roll back to the A string as you set your 1st finger and High 2 C ♯, play two long bows, followed by a very long C ♯ up bow.

mm9. Remove your 2nd finger and play four long B's, starting down bow.

mm10. Play another B with a long down bow. Set your High 2 and play a long up bow C ♯. Set your 3rd finger and play a very long D, using the full length of your down bow.

mm11. Remove your 3rd finger and play four long C ♯'s, starting up bow.

mm12. Play another C ♯ with a long up bow and set your 3rd finger to play a long down bow D. Remove all fingers and roll over to the Open E string, and play a very long E, the full length of your up bow.

mm13. Play a long Open E, down bow. Roll over to the A string, set down your High 2 C ♯, and play three long C ♯'s, starting up bow.

mm14. Hold your High 2, and set down your 1st and 3rd finger on the A string. Play a long down bow on 3rd finger D, and then remove your 3rd and 2nd finger to play 1st finger B with three long bows, starting up bow.

mm15. Remove your 1st finger and play an Open A with a long down bow. Set your High 2 C ♯ and play a long up bow. Roll over to the Open E string as you remove your High 2, and play Open E with two long bows.

mm16. Roll back to the A string as you set your 1st finger and High 2 C ♯, and play two long bows, followed by a very long C ♯, using the full length of your down bow.

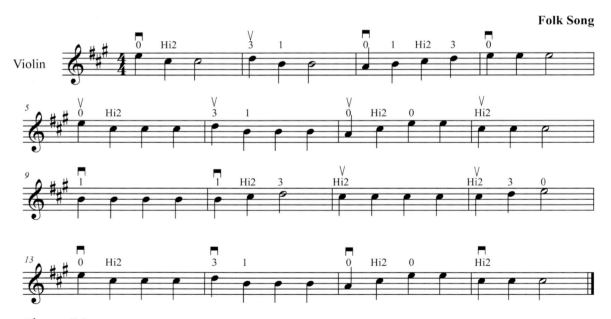

Figure 7.2
Lightly Row

Song of the Wind

Basic song characteristics:

- ✍ **Metronome: Quarter note = 72.**

- ✍ **Key signature: A Major, three sharps: F♯, C♯, and G♯.**

- ✍ **Time signature: Simple, four beats per measure and the quarter note gets the beat. Whole note = 4 beats, half note = 2 beats, quarter note = 1 beat.**

- ✍ **Strings: A string = High 2 finger pattern, E string = High 2 finger pattern.**

- ✍ **Note names, first line: A, B, C♯, D // E, E, E, E // F♯, D, A, F♯ // E, quarter rest, quarter rest//.**

- ✍ **Rhythm, first line: Long-long-long-long // long-long-long-long // long-long-long-long // very long-rest-rest//.**

- ✍ **Fingering technical difficulty: Holding 1st finger F♯ while you cross your bow and 3rd finger D to the A string, hop the 3rd finger over to the A and roll your bow to the E string (measures 3 and 5).**

- ✍ **Bowing technical difficulty: To reset, play the first down bow and then lift your bow in the air and reset it at the frog of the bow (measures 4, 6, and 10).**

- ✍ **See the DVD for a performance of the song with the metronome.**

Here's how to play the song measure by measure:

mm1. Place your bow near the lower half on the Open A string and play a High 2 finger pattern, starting down bow.

mm2. Remove all fingers and roll over to the E string to play four long Open E's, starting down bow.

mm3. Set your 1st finger F♯ on the E string and play a long down bow. Hold your 1st finger on the E string while you cross your 3rd finger D to the A string, roll your bow to the A string a play a long up bow. Hop your 3rd finger A to the E string, roll your bow to the E string, and play a long down bow. Remove your 3rd finger, your 1st finger F should still be holding on the E string, and play a long up bow.

mm4. Remove your 1st finger and play a very long Open E, using the full length of your down bow. Reset your bow back to the frog, or lower half, as you rest for two beats.

mm5. Set your 1st finger F♯ on the E string and play a long down bow. Hold your 1st finger on the E string while you cross your 3rd finger D to the A string, roll your bow to the A string and play a long up bow. Hop your 3rd finger A to the E string, roll your bow to the E string, and play a long down bow. Remove your 3rd finger—your 1st finger F should still be holding the E string—and play a long up bow.

mm6. Remove your 1st finger and play a very long Open E, using the full length of your down bow. Reset your bow back to the frog as you rest for two beats.

mm7. Play another Open E with a long down bow. Roll over to the A string and set down your 1st, 2nd, and 3rd fingers D. Play three long D's, starting up bow.

mm8. Continue the musical phrase and play another long down bow D. Remove your 3rd finger to play High 2 C♯ three times with long bows, starting up bow.

mm9. Continue the musical phrase and play another long down bow C♯. Remove your 2nd finger to play 1st finger B three times with long bows, starting up bow.

mm10. Remove your first finger B to play Open A with a long down bow. Set your High 2 C♯ and play a long up bow. Remove all fingers and roll over to the E string to play a long down bow, Open E. Stop and reset your bow to the frog, or lower half, as you rest for one beat.

mm11. Play another Open E with a long down bow. Roll over to the A string and set down your 1st, 2nd, and 3rd fingers D. Play three long D's, starting up bow.

mm12. Continue the musical phrase and play another long down bow D. Remove your 3rd finger to play High 2 C♯ three times with long bows, starting up bow.

mm13. Continue the musical phrase and play another long down bow C♯. Remove your 2nd finger to play 1st finger B three times with long bows, starting up bow.

mm14. Remove your 1st finger B to play a very-very-very-long Open A, using the full length of your slow down bow.

Folk Song

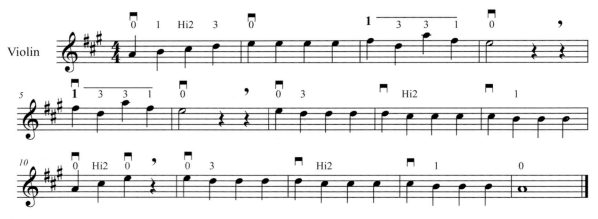

Figure 7.3
Song of the Wind

Go Tell Aunt Rhody

Basic song characteristics:

- ❧ **Metronome: Quarter note = 50.**

- ❧ **Key signature: A Major, three sharps: F♯, C♯, and G♯.**

- ❧ **Time signature: Simple, four beats per measure and the quarter note gets the beat. Half note = 2 beats, quarter note = 1 beat, eighth note = ½ beat.**

- ❧ **Strings: A string = High 2 finger pattern, E string = High 2 finger pattern.**

- ❧ **Note names, first line: C♯, C♯, B, A, A // B, B, C♯, B, A // E, E, D, C♯, C♯ // B, A, B, C♯, A//.**

- ❧ **Rhythm, first line: Long-short-short-long-long // long-long-short-short-long // long-short-short-long-long // short-short-short-short-very long//.**

- ❧ **Fingering technical difficulty: Going from the Open E string to 3rd finger D, by quickly moving the bow to the A string and setting down your 1, High 2, and 3 (measures 3, 6, and 11).**

- ❧ **Bowing technical difficulty: To bow a long down bow, and then to play the short notes at only the tip of the bow.**

- ❧ **See the DVD for a performance of the song with the metronome.**

Here's how to play the song measure by measure:

mm1. Place your bow near the lower half on the A string as you set your 1st finger and High 2 C♯. Play a long down bow C♯, followed by a short up bow C♯ at the tip of the bow.

Remove the 2nd finger and play a short down bow B at the upper half of the bow. Remove the 1st finger, and play two long Open A's, starting up bow.

mm2. Set your 1st finger B on the A string and play two long B's, starting up bow. Set your High 2 C♯, and play a short up bow C♯ at the tip of the bow. Remove the second finger and play a short down bow B at the tip of the bow. Remove the 1st finger, and play a long up bow Open A.

mm3. Roll over to the E string, and play a long down bow Open E, followed by a short up bow E at the tip of the bow. Quickly roll over to the A string, set your 1st, 2nd, and 3rd fingers, and play a short down bow D at the tip of the bow. Remove the 3rd finger and play two long High 2 C♯'s, starting up bow.

mm4. Remove the 2nd finger and play at the tip a short up bow 1st finger B, a short down bow Open A, a short up bow 1st finger B, and a short down bow High 2 C♯. Remove all fingers and play a very long Open A, using the full length of the up bow.

mm5. Set your 1st and High 2 C♯ and play a long down bow C♯, followed by a short up bow C♯ at the tip of the bow. Set the 3rd finger and play a short down bow D at the tip of the bow. Roll over to the E string as you remove all fingers, and play two long E's, starting up bow.

mm6. Set your 1st finger F♯ on the E string and play two long F♯'s starting up bow. Remove your 1st finger and play a short down bow Open E at the tip of the bow. Quickly roll over to the A string, set the 1st, 2nd, and 3rd fingers, and play a short down bow D at the tip of the bow. Remove the 3rd finger and play a long up bow C♯.

mm7. Continue the musical phrase by playing another long down bow High 2 C♯, followed by a short up bow C♯ at the tip of the bow. Set the 3rd finger and play a short down bow D at the tip of the bow. Roll over to the E string as you remove all fingers, and play two long E's, starting up bow.

mm8. Set your 1st finger F♯ on the E string and play two long F♯'s, starting up bow. Remove your 1st finger and play a very long Open E using the full length of your up bow.

mm9. Roll over to the A string and set your 1st finger and High 2 C♯. Play a long down bow C♯, followed by a short up bow C♯ at the tip of the bow. Remove the 2nd finger and

play a short down bow B at the tip of the bow. Remove the 1st finger, and play two long Open A's, starting up bow.

mm10. Set your 1st finger B on the A string and play two long B's, starting up bow. Set your High 2 C♯, and play a short up bow C♯ at the tip of the bow. Remove the 2nd finger and play a short down bow B at the tip of the bow. Remove the 1st finger and play a long up bow Open A.

mm11. Roll over to the E string, and play a long down bow Open E, followed by a short up bow E at the tip of the bow. Quickly roll over to the A string, set your 1st, 2nd, and 3rd fingers, and play a short down bow D at the tip of the bow. Remove the 3rd finger and play two long High 2 C♯'s, starting up bow.

mm12. Remove the 2nd finger and play at the tip a short up bow 1st finger B, a short down bow Open A, a short up bow 1st finger B, and a short down bow High 2 C♯. Remove all fingers and play a very long Open A, using the full length of the up bow.

Figure 7.4
Go Tell Aunt Rhody

Ode to Joy

Basic song characteristics:

- Metronome: Quarter note = 72.

- Key signature: D Major, two sharps: F♯ and C♯.

- Time signature: Simple, four beats per measure and the quarter note gets the beat. Half note = 2 beats, dotted quarter note = 1 ½ beats, quarter note = 1 beat, eighth note = ½ beat.

- Strings: D string = High 2 finger pattern, A string = High 2 finger pattern.

- Note names, first line: C♯, C♯, D, E // E, D, C♯, B // A, A, B, C♯ // C♯, B, B//

- Rhythm, first line: Long-long-long-long // long-long-long-long // long-long-long-long // dotted-short-very long//.

- Fingering technical difficulty: To use 4th finger E instead of Open E string (measures 1, 2, 5, 6, 13, and 14).

- Bowing technical difficulty: To use a small amount of bow on the long dotted quarter note, and to use a fast bow on the short eighth note in order to have enough bow left over for the very long half note.

- See the DVD for a performance of the song with the metronome.

Here's how to play the song measure by measure:

mm1. Place your bow near the lower half on the A string and set your 1st finger and High 2 C♯. Play two long C♯'s, starting down bow. Set the 3rd finger and play a long down bow D. Set the 4th finger and play a long up bow E.

mm2. Continue the musical phrase and play another 4th finger E on the A string with a long down bow. Remove the 4th finger and play a long up bow 3rd finger D. Remove the 3rd finger and play a long down bow High 2 C♯. Remove the 2nd finger and play a long up bow 1st finger B.

mm3. Remove the 1st finger and play two long Open A's, starting down bow. Set the 1st finger and play a long down bow B. Set the High 2 and play a long up bow C♯.

mm4. Continue the music phrase by playing another High 2 C♯ with a long down bow moving at a slow speed. Remove the 2nd finger and play a short up bow B moving at a quick speed, followed by a very long B using the full length of the down bow.

mm5. Set your 1st finger and High 2 C♯. Play two long C♯'s, starting up bow. Set the 3rd finger and play a long up bow D. Set the 4th finger and play a long down bow E.

mm6.   Continue the musical phrase and play another 4th finger E on the A string with a long up bow. Remove the 4th finger and play a long down bow 3rd finger D. Remove the 3rd finger and play a long up bow High 2 C ♯. Remove the 2nd finger and play a long down bow 1st finger B.

mm7.   Remove the 1st finger and play two long Open A's, starting up bow. Set the 1st finger and play a long up bow B. Set the High 2 and play a long down bow C ♯.

mm8.   Remove the 2nd finger and play the 1st finger B with a long up bow moving at a slow speed. Remove the 1st finger and play a short down bow Open A moving at a quick speed, followed by a very long Open A using the full length of the up bow.

mm9.   Set the 1st finger B and play two B's, starting down bow. Set the High 2 and play a long down bow C ♯. Remove all fingers and play a long up bow Open A.

mm10.   Set the 1st finger and play a long down bow B. Set the High 2 and play a short up bow C ♯ at the tip of the bow. Set the 3rd finger and play a short down bow at the tip of the bow. Remove the 3rd finger and play a long up bow C ♯. Remove all fingers and play a long down bow Open A.

mm11.   Set the 1st finger and play a long up bow B. Set the High 2 and play a short down bow C ♯ at the tip of the bow. Set the 3rd finger and play a short up bow at the tip of the bow. Remove the 3rd finger and play a long down bow C ♯. Remove the 2nd finger and play a long up bow 1st finger B.

mm12.   Remove the 1st finger and play a long down bow Open A. Set the 1st finger and play a long up bow B. Hop the 1st finger to the D string and roll the bow to the D string, and play a very long E, using the full length of the down bow.

mm13.   Roll back to the A string and set your 1st finger and High 2 C ♯. Play two long C ♯'s, starting up bow. Set the 3rd finger and play a long up bow D. Set the 4th finger and play a long down bow E.

mm14.   Continue the musical phrase and play another 4th finger E on the A string with a long up bow. Remove the 4th finger and play a long down bow 3rd finger D. Remove the 3rd finger and play a long up bow High 2 C ♯. Remove the 2nd finger and play a long down bow 1st finger B.

mm15.   Remove the 1st finger and play two long Open A's, starting up bow. Set the 1st finger and play a long up bow B. Set the High 2 and play a long down bow C ♯.

mm16.   Remove the 2nd finger and play the 1st finger B with a long up bow moving at a slow speed. Remove the 1st finger and play a short down bow Open A, moving at a quick speed, followed by a very long Open A using the full length of the up bow.

Beethoven

Figure 7.5
Ode to Joy

🎵 ♪ ♩ 🎵 ♪ ♩ 🎵 ♪ ♩

"I started playing piano at age 4, and while I was watching my first grade talent show, I knew I wanted to play the violin. So my mom signed me up for violin lessons. I love anything to do with music, like playing music and listening to music. So, now I am playing both the violin and piano."

—Shreya, 9 years old

Yellow Rose of Texas

Basic song characteristics:

- Metronome: Quarter note = 96.

- Key signature: D Major, two sharps: F♯ and C♯.

- Time signature: Simple, four beats per measure and the quarter note gets the beat. Whole note = 4 beats, dotted half note = 3 beats, half note = 2 beats, quarter note = 1 beat.

- Strings: D string = High 2 finger pattern, A string = High 2 finger pattern, E string = Low 2 finger pattern.

- Note names, first phrase: Rest, rest, A, G // F♯, A, A, A // B, A, G // F♯, A, D, E // F♯, E//

- Rhythm, first phrase: Quarter rest-quarter rest-long-long // long-long-long-long // long-very long- long // long-long-long-long // very very long-long//.

- Fingering technical difficulty: Prep the 3rd finger G and the High 2 F♯ on the D string before starting the song (measure 1). Hold the 1st finger F♯ on the E string while you roll the bow to the A string to play Open A (measures 5, 6, and 13). After holding the 1st finger F♯ on the E string, set the Low 2 on the red tape for the note G natural (measure 14).

- See the DVD for a performance of the song with the metronome.

> "Playing the violin helped me judge when a football is going to be low enough for me to catch by improving my timing though all of the counting and rhythm exercises on my violin solos."
>
> —Kevin, 10 years old

Here's how to play the song measure by measure:

mm1. Hover your High 2 and 3rd finger over your D string. Place your bow on Open A and play a long down bow. Roll over to the D string and set your High 2 and 3rd finger, and play a long up bow G.

mm2. Continue the musical phrase by removing the 3rd finger and playing a long down bow High 2 C♯. Roll over to the A string and play three long Open A's, starting up bow.

mm3. Set your 1st finger on the A string and play a long down bow B. Remove your 1st finger to play a very long up bow Open A. Roll over to the D string as you set your 1st, 2nd, and 3rd fingers, and play a long down bow G.

mm4. Remove your 3rd finger to play a High 2 F♯ with a long up bow. Roll over to the A string and play a long down bow Open A. Quickly set your 1st, 2nd, and 3rd fingers and play a long up bow D. Roll over to the E string and play a long down bow E.

mm5.   Set your 1ˢᵗ finger F♯ on the E string, and play a very-very-long F♯ using the full up bow. Hold your 1ˢᵗ finger on the E string and roll the bow to the A string to play a long down bow A.

mm6.   Continue the musical phrase and play another long up bow Open A. Roll back to the E string, and your 1ˢᵗ finger F♯ should still be pressed on the string. Play three long F♯'s, starting down bow.

mm7.   Continue the musical phrase and play another long up bow F♯. Remove your 1ˢᵗ finger to play a very long down bow Open E. Roll over to the A string, set your 1ˢᵗ, 2ⁿᵈ, and 3ʳᵈ fingers, and play a long up bow D.

mm8.   Remove your 3ʳᵈ finger and play the High 2 C with a long down bow. Set your 3ʳᵈ finger, and play a long up bow D. Roll over to the E string, and play a long down bow E. Set your 1ˢᵗ finger on the E string, and play a long up bow F♯.

mm9.   Remove the 1ˢᵗ finger to play an Open E with a very-very-long down bow using the full length of the bow. Roll over to the D string and set your 1ˢᵗ, 2ⁿᵈ, and 3ʳᵈ finger. Play a long up bow on 3ʳᵈ finger G.

mm10. Remove the 3ʳᵈ finger and play a long down bow High 2 F♯. Roll over to the A string and play three long Open A's, starting up bow.

mm11. Set your 1ˢᵗ finger on the A string and play a long down bow B. Remove your 1ˢᵗ finger to play two long Open A's, starting up bow. Roll over to the D string as you set your 1ˢᵗ, 2ⁿᵈ, and 3ʳᵈ finger, and play a long up bow G.

mm12. Remove your 3ʳᵈ finger to play High 2 F♯ with a long down bow. Roll over to the A string and play a long up bow Open A. Quickly set your 1ˢᵗ, 2ⁿᵈ, and 3ʳᵈ fingers and play a long down bow D. Roll over to the E string and play a long up bow E.

mm13. Set your 1ˢᵗ finger F♯ on the E string, and play a very-very-long F♯ using the full down bow. Hold your 1ˢᵗ finger on the E string and roll the bow to the A string to play a long up bow A.

mm14. Continue the musical phrase and play another long down bow Open A. Roll back to the E string, and your 1ˢᵗ finger F♯ should still be pressed on the string. Set your Low 2 G on the red tape, next to your 1ˢᵗ finger, and play three long G's, starting up bow.

mm15. Continue the musical phrase and play another long down bow G. Remove the 2ⁿᵈ finger and play 1ˢᵗ finger F♯ with a long up bow. Remove the 1ˢᵗ finger to play a long down bow Open E. Roll over to the A string and set your 1ˢᵗ 2ⁿᵈ and 3ʳᵈ fingers. Play a long up bow D.

mm16. Continue the musical phrase and play another long down bow D. Remove all fingers and play a long up bow Open A. Roll over to the E string and set your 1ˢᵗ finger, and play a long down bow F♯. Remove the 1ˢᵗ finger to play a long up bow Open E.

mm17. Roll over to the A string, and set your 1ˢᵗ, 2ⁿᵈ, and 3ʳᵈ fingers D. Play a very-very-very-long 3ʳᵈ finger D using the full length of the down bow.

Figure 7.6
Yellow Rose of Texas

"I decided I wanted to play the violin because it looked cool and I liked the way it sounded. Mrs. Seidel makes learning the violin easy."

—Darcey, 8 years old

On Top of Old Smoky

Basic song characteristics:

- ✍ Metronome: Quarter note = 96.
- ✍ Key Signature: C Major, no sharps or flats.
- ✍ Time Signature: Simple, three beats per measure and the quarter note gets the beat. Dotted half note = 3 beats, half note = 2 beats, quarter note = 1 beat.
- ✍ Strings: D string = Low 2 finger pattern, A string = Low 2 finger pattern, E string = Low 1 finger pattern.
- ✍ Note names, first line: Rest, rest, G // G, B, D // G, E // E, E // C, E, G // D//.
- ✍ Rhythm, first line: Quarter rest-quarter rest-long // long-long-long // long-very long// very long-long// long-long-long // very very long//.
- ✍ Fingering technical difficulty: Prep the 1st finger B on the A string before crossing over the 3rd finger G on the D string (measure 1). Hold the Low 2 G on the E string while you cross over 3rd finger D to the A string (measures 6, 7, 17, and 18).
- ✍ Bowing technical difficulty: The half note slurs E's will merge together to become one whole note E that lasts four beats (measures 3, 4, 9, 10, 15, 16, 21, and 22). Double ups, play the first up bow with a slow bow and stop in the middle of the bow, rest, and then play the second up bow in the lower half of the bow (measures 6, 7, 12, 13, 18, and 19).
- ✍ See the DVD for a performance of the song with the metronome.

Here's how to play the song measure by measure:

mm1. Set your 1st finger B on the A string, and then cross over your 3rd finger G to the D string. Place your bow near the middle of the bow and play a long up bow G.

mm2. Continue the musical phrase and play another long 3rd finger G down bow. Roll to the A string and your 1st finger B should be already on the string. Play a long up bow B. Set your 3rd finger, and play a long down bow D.

mm3. Roll to the E string and set your Low 2 on the red tape, and play a long up bow G. Remove the 2nd finger to play a very-very-very-long Open E, using the full length of the down bow.

mm4. After you slur both two-beat Open E's together, play another long up bow Open E.

mm5. Roll to the A string, set your Low 2 on the red tape, and play a long down bow C. Roll back to the E string, and play a long up bow Open E. Set your Low 2 on the red tape, and play a long down bow G.

mm6. Hold your Low 2 G on the E string as you roll to the A string and cross your 3rd finger over to the A string. Play a very-very-long 3rd finger D, using a slow up bow until the middle of the bow.

mm7. As you rest for two beats in the middle of the bow, roll the bow to the D string and hop your 3rd finger to the D string. Continue the up bow, and play a long 3rd finger G.

mm8. Continue the musical phrase and play another long 3rd finger G down bow. Roll to the A string, set your 1st finger, and play a long up bow B. Set your 3rd finger, and play a long down bow D.

mm9. Continue the musical phrase and play another long 3rd finger D up bow. Remove the 3rd finger to play a very-very-very-long Open A, using the full length of the down bow.

mm10. After you slur both two-beat Open A's together, set your 1st finger, and play a long up bow B.

mm11. Set your Low 2 on the red tape and play a long down bow C. Remove your 2nd finger, and play a long up bow 1st finger B. Remove your 1st finger, and play a long down bow Open A.

mm12. Roll to the D string and set your 1st, 2nd, and 3rd fingers G. Play a very-very-long up bow, using a slow bow until the middle of the bow.

mm13. Rest for two beats, and play another long up bow 3rd finger G.

mm14. Continue the musical phrase and play another long 3rd finger G down bow. Roll to the A string, set your 1st finger, and play a long up bow B. Set your 3rd finger, and play a long down bow D.

mm15. Roll to the E string and set your Low 2 on the red tape, and play a long up bow G. Remove the 2nd finger to play a very-very-very-long Open E, using the full length of the down bow.

mm16. After you slur both two-beat Open E's together, play another long up bow Open E.

mm17. Roll to the A string, set your Low 2 on the red tape, and play a long down bow C. Roll back to the E string and play a long up bow Open E. Set your Low 2 on the red tape and play a long down bow G.

mm18. Hold your Low 2 G on the E string as you roll to the A string and cross your 3rd finger over to the A string. Play a very-very-long 3rd finger D, using a slow up bow until the middle of the bow.

mm19. As you rest for two beats in the middle of the bow, roll the bow to the D string and hop your 3rd finger to the D string. Continue the up bow, and play a long 3rd finger G.

mm20. Continue the musical phrase and play another long 3rd finger G down bow. Roll to the A string, set your 1st finger, and play a long up bow B. Set your 3rd finger, and play a long down bow D.

mm21. Continue the musical phrase and play another long 3rd finger D up bow. Remove the 3rd finger to play a very-very-very-long Open A, using the full length of the down bow.

mm22. After you slur both two-beat Open A's together, set your 1st finger, and play a long up bow B.

mm23. Set your Low 2 on the red tape and play a
long down bow C. Remove your 2nd finger
and play a long up bow 1st finger B.
Remove your 1st finger and play a long
down bow Open A.

mm24. Roll to the D string and set your 1st, 2nd,
and 3rd finger G. Play a very-very-long up
bow, using the full length of the bow.

Folk Song

Figure 7.7
On Top of Old Smoky

Minuet in C

Basic song characteristics:

- Metronome: Quarter note = 56.

- Key signature: C Major, no sharps or flats.

- Time signature: Simple, three beats per measure and the quarter note gets the beat. Dotted half note = 3 beats, half note = 2 beats, quarter note = 1 beat, eighth note = ½ beat.

- Strings: G string = High 2 finger pattern, D string = Low 2 finger pattern, A string = Low 2 finger pattern.

- Repeat measure marking: Play measures 1–8, reset the bow, and play measures 1–8 again before continuing through the remainder of the song.

- Note names, first phrase: G, G, G // E, D, E, C// D, G, F // E, D // G, F, E, D, C // A F, E, D, C // B, A, G, B // C//.

- Rhythm, first phrase: Long-long-long // long-short-short-long // long-long-long // very long-long // long-short-short-short-short // long-short-short-short-short // long-short-short-long // very very long//.

- Fingering technical difficulty: Use the 3rd finger C that is holding on the G string to help set your 4th finger A on the upper D string (measures 5, 6, 21, and 22). The accidental F♯ will affect all F's to become F♯'s in the measure; once the measure is completed with the bar line, refer back to the key signature (measures 10, 12, and 15).

- Bowing technical difficulty: The up bow slurs are performed with staccato, which means to perform two separate up bows by stopping in the middle of the bow before performing the second note in the staccato slur (measures 1, 3, and 15). Resets between the two down bows in a row (measures 8, and 16).

- See the DVD for a performance of the song with the metronome.

Here's how to play the song measure by measure:

mm1. Place your bow on the D string near the middle of the bow. Set your 1st, 2nd, and 3rd fingers on the D string. Play a long 3rd finger G down bow, until the tip of the bow. Continue the music phrase and play two more long up bow G's in a slur. You do this by playing the first long G up bow and stopping in the middle, and then playing the second long G up bow until the frog of the bow.

mm2. Remove the 3rd and 2nd finger to play a long down bow 1st finger E. Remove the 1st finger and play a short up bow Open D at the tip of the bow. Set your 1st finger again and play a short down bow E at the tip of the bow. Hold the 1st finger as your roll to the G string and cross over your 3rd finger to play a long up bow C.

mm3. Remove all fingers, and roll to the D string to play a long down bow Open D. Quickly set your 1st, Low 2, and 3rd fingers to play a long up bow G that is staccato slurred to a long up bow Low 2 F. To do this slur, play the first long up bow, stop in the middle, remove the 3rd finger, and play another long up bow.

mm4. Remove the 2nd finger and play a very long down bow 1st finger E, using the full length of the bow. Remove the 1st finger and play a long up bow Open D.

mm5. Quickly set your 1st, Low 2, and 3rd fingers to play a long down bow G. Remove your 3rd finger and play a short up bow Low 2 F at the tip of the bow. Remove your 2nd finger and play a short down bow 1st finger E at the tip of the bow. Remove your 1st finger and play a short up bow Open D at the tip of the bow. Roll over to the G string and cross over your 3rd finger to play a short down bow C at the tip of the bow.

mm6. Hold your 3rd finger on the G string as you place your 4th finger on the D string and roll your bow to the D string. Play a long up bow 4th finger A. Set your 1st and Low 2 on the D string, and play a short down bow F at the frog of the bow. Remove your 2nd finger and play a short up bow 1st finger E at the frog of the bow. Remove your 1st finger and play a short down bow Open D at the frog of the bow. Roll over to the G string and cross over your 3rd finger to play a short up bow C at the frog of the bow.

mm7. Set your 1st and High 2 on the G string, and play a long down bow B. Remove your 2nd finger and play a short up bow 1st finger A at the tip of the bow. Remove your 1st finger and play a short down bow Open G at the tip of the bow. Quickly set your 1st and High 2 and play a long up bow B.

mm8. Set your third finger and play a very-very-long C, using the full length of the down bow. Stop and reset the bow to play another down bow. On the first time playing this song, repeat mm 1–8.

mm9. Set your 1st finger on the D string and play a long down bow E. Roll to the A string and play a very long up bow Open A, using the full length of the bow.

mm10. Roll back to the D string, set your 1st and High 2, and play a long down bow F♯. Remove your 2nd finger and play a short up bow 1st finger E at the tip of the bow. Set your High 2 and play a short down bow F♯ at the tip of the bow. Remove all fingers and play a long up bow Open D.

mm11. Set your 1st, 2nd, and 3rd finger, and play a long down bow G. Remove all fingers, roll to the A string, and play a long up bow Open A. Set your 1st finger and play a long down bow B.

mm12. Remove your 1st finger and play a short up bow Open A at the tip of your bow. Roll to the D string, set your 1st, High 2, and 3rd finger, and play a short down bow G. Remove your 3rd finger and play a short up bow F♯. Remove your 2nd finger and play a short down bow E. Remove your 1st finger, and play a long up bow Open D.

mm13. Roll to the A string and set your 1st, Low 2, and 3rd finger, to play a long down bow D. Remove your 3rd finger, and play a short up bow Low 2 C at the tip of the bow. Remove your 2nd finger, and play a short down bow B. Remove your 1st finger, and play a short up bow Open A. Roll to the D string and quickly set your 1st, High 2, and 3rd finger to play a short down bow G at the tip of the bow.

mm14. Hold the 3rd finger on the D string as you place your 4th finger on the A string. Roll the bow to the A string and play a long up bow 4th finger A. Remove your 4th finger, set your 1st and Low 2, and play a short down bow C at the frog of the bow. Remove your 2nd finger and play a short up bow B. Remove your 1st finger and play a short down bow Open A. Roll to the D string, set your 1st, High 2, and 3rd fingers, and play a short up bow G.

mm15. Remove your 3rd finger and play a long down bow F ♯. Remove all fingers and play a long up bow Open D, using only half of the bow. Stop the bow, set your High 2 again, and play a long up bow F ♯ using the other half of the bow.

mm16. Set your 3rd finger and play a very-very-long G, using the full length of the down bow. Stop and reset the bow at the frog as you continue to hold your 3rd finger.

mm17. Play a long down bow G. Pull back your 2nd finger to the Low 2 red tape and play a short up bow F at the tip of the bow. Remove your 2nd finger, and play a short down bow 1st finger E. Remove your 1st finger and play a long up bow Open D.

mm18. Set your 1st finger and play a long down bow E. Remove your 1st finger and play a short up bow Open D, at the tip of the bow. Set your 1st finger again and play a short down bow E. Hold your 1st finger as you cross over your 3rd finger to the G string. Roll your bow to the G string and play a long 3rd finger C.

mm19. Roll to the D string, set your 1st and Low 2, and play a very long down bow F. Continue the music phrase and play a short up bow F at the tip of the bow. Remove the 2nd finger and play a short down bow 1st finger E.

mm20. Remove your 1st finger and play a very-very-long Open D, using the full length of the up bow.

mm21. Quickly set your 1st, Low 2, and 3rd finger to play a long down bow G. Remove your 3rd finger and play a short up bow Low 2 F at the tip of the bow. Remove your 2nd finger and play a short down bow 1st finger E at the tip of the bow. Remove your 1st finger and play a short up bow Open D at the tip of the bow. Roll over to the G string and cross over your 3rd finger to play a short down bow C at the tip of the bow.

mm22. Hold your 3rd finger on the G string as you place your 4th finger on the D string and roll your bow to the D string. Play a long up bow 4th finger A. Set your 1st and Low 2 on the D string and play a short down bow F at the frog of the bow. Remove your 2nd finger and play a short up bow 1st finger E at the frog of the bow. Remove your 1st finger, and play a short down bow Open D, at the frog of the bow. Roll over to the G string and cross over your 3rd finger to play a short up bow C, at the frog of the bow.

mm23. Set your 1st and High 2 on the G string and play a long down bow B. Remove your 2nd finger and play a short up bow 1st finger A at the tip of the bow. Remove your 1st finger, and play a short down bow Open G at the tip of the bow. Quickly set your 1st and High 2 and play a long up bow B.

mm24. Set your 3rd finger and play a very-very-long C, using the full length of the down bow.

J.S. Bach

Figure 7.8
Minuet in C

Minuet in G

Basic song characteristics:

- ✒ Metronome: Quarter note = 60.

- ✒ Key signature: G Major, one sharp: F♯.

- ✒ Time signature: Simple, three beats per measure and the quarter note gets the beat. Dotted half note = 3 beats, quarter note = 1 beat, eighth note = ½ beat.

- ✒ Strings: D string = High 2 finger pattern, A string = Low 2 finger pattern, E string = Low 2 finger pattern.

- ✒ Repeat measure marking: Play measures 1–16, reset the bow, and play measures 1-16 again before continuing through the remainder of the song.

- ✒ Note names, first phrase: D, G, A, B, C // D, G, G // E, C, D, E, F♯ // G, G, G // C, D, C, B, A // B, C, B, A, G // F♯, G, A B, G // B, A//.

- ✒ Rhythm, first phrase: Long-short-short-short-short // long-long-long // long-short-short-short-short // long-long-long // long-short-short-short-short // long-short-short-short-short // long-short-short-short-short // grace-very very long//.

- ✒ Fingering technical difficulty: Use the 3rd finger G that is holding on the D string to help set your 4th finger E on the upper A string (measures 2, 3, 10, 11, 25, and 26). The accidental C♯ will affect all C's to become C♯'s in the measure. Once the measure is completed with the bar line, refer back to the key signature (measures 20, 21, and 23).

- ✒ The grace note B will be performed as a tiny, or extremely short, 1st finger B that is slurred to a half note Open A (measure 8).

- ✒ Bowing technical difficulty: Smooth slurs connecting both short eighth notes together in the same bow direction (measure 1), and staccato slurs separating the two long quarter notes in the same bow direction (measure 2). Resets between the two down bows in a row (measures 8, 16, and 24).

- ✒ See the DVD for a performance of the song with the metronome.

Here's how to play the song measure by measure:

mm1. Place your bow on the A string near the middle of the bow. Set your 1st, Low 2, and 3rd finger on the A string. Play a long down bow 3rd finger D. Roll the bow and hop your 3rd finger to the D string to play an up bow G that is continuously slurred with an Open A. Set your 1st finger, and play a short down bow B near the middle of the bow. Set your Low 2 and play a short up bow C, near the middle of the bow.

mm2. Set your 3rd finger and play a long down bow D. Hop your 3rd finger to the D string and roll your bow to the D string to play two up bow staccato G's.

mm3. Hold your 3rd finger on the D string, as you place your 4th finger on the A string. Roll your bow to the A string and play a long down bow 4th finger E. Set your 1st and Low 2 on the A string and play an up bow C that is continuously slurred with a 3rd finger D. Remove all fingers and roll to the E string and play a short down bow E near the middle of the bow. Set your 1st finger and play a short up bow F ♯ near the middle of the bow.

mm4. Set your Low 2 and play a long down bow G. Hold the Low 2 and cross your 3rd finger to the D string to play two up bow staccato slurred G's.

mm5. Hop your Low 2 to the A string and roll your bow to the A string to play a long down bow C. Set your 3rd finger and continuously slur up bow D with your Low 2 C. Remove your 2nd finger and play a short down bow B near the middle of your bow. Remove your 1st finger and play a short up bow Open A near the middle of your bow.

mm6. Set your 1st finger and play a long down bow B. Set your Low 2 and play an up bow C that is continuously slurred with a 1st finger B. Remove your 1st finger and play a short down bow Open A. Roll to the D string and set your 1st High 2 and 3rd finger to play a short up bow G.

mm7. Remove your 3rd finger and play a long down bow High 2 F ♯. Set your 3rd finger to play an up bow G that is continuously slurred with an Open A. Set your 1st finger and play a short down bow B near the middle of the bow. Hold your B as you cross your 3rd finger to the D string. Roll your bow to the D string and play a short up bow G.

mm8. Roll back to the A string and your 1st finger should still be holding. Play a down bow grace note B that is continuously slurred with a very-very-long Open A. Stop and reset your bow.

mm9. Set your 1st Low 2 and 3rd finger on the A string. Play a long down bow 3rd finger D. Roll the bow and hop your 3rd finger to the D string to play an up bow G that is continuously slurred with an Open A. Set your 1st finger and play a short down bow B near the middle of the bow. Set your Low 2 and play a short up bow C near the middle of the bow.

mm10. Set your 3rd finger and play a long down bow D. Hop your 3rd finger to the D string and roll your bow to the D string to play two up bow staccato G's.

mm11. Hold your 3rd finger on the D string as you place your 4th finger on the A string. Roll your bow to the A string and play a long down bow 4th finger E. Set your 1st and Low 2 on the A string and play an up bow C that is continuously slurred with a 3rd finger D. Remove all fingers and roll to the E string and play a short down bow E near the middle of the bow. Set your 1st finger and play a short up bow F ♯ near the middle of the bow.

mm12. Set your Low 2 and play a long down bow G. Hold the Low 2 and cross your 3rd finger to the D string to play two up bow staccato slurred G's.

mm13. Hop your Low 2 to the A string and roll your bow to the A string to play a long down bow C. Set your 3rd finger and continuously slur up bow D with your Low 2 C. Remove your 2nd finger and play a short down bow B near the middle of your bow. Remove your 1st finger and play a short up bow Open A near the middle of your bow.

mm14. Set your 1st finger and play a long down bow B. Set your Low 2 and play an up bow C that is continuously slurred with a 1st finger B. Remove your 1st finger and play a short down bow Open A. Roll to the D string and set your 1st High 2 and 3rd finger to play a short up bow G.

mm15. Roll back to the A string and play a long down bow Open A. Set your 1st finger and play an up bow B that is continuously slurred with an Open A. Roll to the D string and set your 1st High 2 and 3rd fingers to play a short down bow G. Remove your 3rd finger and play a short High 2 F ♯.

mm16. Set your 3rd finger and play a very-very-long G using the full length of the down bow. Stop and reset the bow to the frog. On the first time playing this song repeat mm 1–16.

mm17. Roll to the E string and set your 1st Low 2 3rd, and 4th fingers. Play a long down bow 4th finger B. Remove your 4th and 3rd fingers to play an up bow G that is continuously slurred with a 3rd finger A. Set your 4th finger and play a short down bow B. Remove your 4th and 3rd fingers and play a short up bow Low 2 G.

mm18. Set your 3rd finger and play a long down bow A. Hop your 3rd finger to the A string and roll your bow to the A string to play an up bow D that is continuously slurred with an Open E. Set your 1st finger and play a short down bow F ♯. Hold your 1st finger while you cross over your 3rd finger to the A string to play a short up bow D.

mm19. Roll back to the E string and set your Low 2 to play a long down bow G. Remove all fingers and play an up bow Open E that is continuously slurred with 1st finger F ♯. Set your 2nd finger and play a short down bow G. Cross over your 3rd finger to the A string and roll your bow to the A string to play a short up bow D.

mm20. Remove your 3rd finger set a High 2 and play a long down bow C ♯. Remove your 2nd finger and play a short up bow 1st finger B. Set your High 2 again and play a short down bow C ♯. Remove all fingers and play a long up bow Open A.

mm21. Continuously slur a down bow Open A with 1st finger B. Set your High 2 and play a short up bow C ♯ at the tip of your bow. Set your 3rd finger and play a short down bow D. Roll to the E string and play a short up bow E. Set your 1st finger and play a short down bow F ♯.

mm22. Set your Low 2 and play a long up bow G. Remove your 2nd finger and play a long down bow F ♯. Remove your 1st finger and play a long up bow Open E.

mm23. Set your 1st finger again and play a long down bow F ♯. Roll over to the A string and play a long up bow Open A that is staccato slurred to a long up bow High 2 C ♯.

mm24. Set your 3rd finger and play a very-very-long D using the full length of the down bow. Stop and reset to the frog of the bow as you continue to hold the 3rd finger.

mm25. Play another long down bow D. Hop your High 2 and 3rd fingers to the D string and roll your bow to the D string to play a short up bow G. Remove your 3rd finger and play a short down bow F ♯. Set your 3rd finger and play a long up bow G.

mm26. Hold your 3rd finger on the D string as you place your 4th finger on the A string. Roll your bow to the A string to play a long down bow 4th finger E. Roll your bow back to the D string and your High 2 and 3rd fingers should still be holding. Play a short up bow G. Remove your 3rd finger and play a short down bow F ♯. Set your 3rd finger and play a long up bow G.

mm27. Hop your 1st Low2 and 3rd finger to the A string and play a long down bow D. Remove your 3rd finger and play a long up bow C that is staccato slurred with a long up bow 1st finger B.

mm28. Remove your 1st finger and play a down bow Open A that is continuously slurred with 3rd finger G. Remove your 3rd finger and play a short up bow High 2 F ♯. Set your 3rd finger and play a short down bow G. Set your 4th finger and play a long up bow A.

mm29. Remove all fingers and play a down bow Open D that is continuously slurred with 1st finger E. Set your High 2 and play a short up bow F ♯ at the tip of the bow. Set your 3rd finger and play a short down bow G. Roll to the A string and play a short up bow Open A. Set your 1st finger and play a short down bow B.

mm30. Set your Low 2 and play a long up bow C. Remove your 2nd finger and play a long down bow B. Remove your 1st finger and play a long up bow Open A.

mm31. Set your 1st finger and play a down bow B that is continuously slurred with 3rd finger D. Hop your High 2 and 3rd finger to the D string and play a long up bow G that is staccato slurred with a long up bow F ♯.

mm32. Set your 3rd finger and play a very-very-long G using the full length of the bow.

Figure 7.9
Minuet in G

Can-Can

Basic song characteristics:

- 🎶 Metronome: Half note = 96.

- 🎶 Key signature: C Major, no sharps or flats.

- 🎶 Time signature: Simple, four beats per measure, and the quarter note gets the beat. Half note = 2 beats, quarter note = 1 beat.

- 🎶 Strings: A string = Low 2 finger pattern, E string = Low 1 finger pattern.

- 🎶 Note names, first line: C, C // D, F, E, D // G, G // G, A, E, F//.

- 🎶 Rhythm, first line: Very long-very long // long-long-long-long // very long-very long // long-long-long-long//.

- 🎶 Fingering technical difficulty: To pull back the Low 1 F on the E string while keeping the 3rd finger on 3rd tape on all strings (measures 2, 4, 6, 8, 10, 12, and 14).

- 🎶 See the DVD for a performance of the song with the metronome.

Here's how to play the song measure by measure:

mm1. Place the lower half of your bow on the A string and set your 1st and Low 2 on the A string. Play a very-long down bow C followed by another very-long up bow C. Both notes will use the full length of the bow.

mm2. Set your 3rd finger and play a long down bow D. Pull back your Low 1 and roll the bow to the E string to play a long up bow F. Remove your 1st finger and play a long down bow Open E. Roll to the A string as you quickly set your 1st, Low 2, and 3rd fingers to play a long up bow D.

mm3. Roll back to the E string and set your Low 1 and Low 2 to play a very-long down bow G followed by another very-long up bow G. Both notes will use the full length of the bow.

mm4. Continue the musical phrase and play a long down bow G. Set your 3rd finger and play a long up bow A. Remove your 3rd finger and play a long down bow Open E. Set your Low 1 and play a long up bow F.

mm5. Hold your Low 1 on the E string while you roll to the A string and set your 3rd finger. Play a very-long down bow D followed by a very-long up bow D. Both notes will use the full length of the bow.

mm6. Set your 3rd finger and play a long down bow D. Remove your 3rd finger roll to the E string and your Low 1 should still be on the E string. Play a long up bow F. Remove your 1st finger and play a long down bow Open E. Roll to the A string as you quickly set your 1st, Low 2, and 3rd fingers to play a long up bow D.

mm7. Remove your 3rd finger and play a long down bow C. Hop your Low 2 over to the E string as you roll your bow to the E string and play a long up bow G followed by another long down bow G. Set your 3rd finger and play a long up bow A.

mm8. Remove your 3rd finger and play a long down bow G. Remove your 2nd finger and play a long up bow Low 1 F. Remove your 1st finger, and play a long Open E. Roll to the A string set your 1st, Low 2, and 3rd fingers to play a long up bow D.

mm9. Remove your 3rd finger and play a very-long down bow C followed by another very-long up bow C. Both notes will use the full length of the bow.

mm10. Set your 3rd finger and play a long down bow D. Pull back your Low 1 and roll the bow to the E string to play a long up bow F. Remove your 1st finger and play a long down bow Open E. Roll to the A string as you quickly set your 1st, Low 2, and 3rd fingers to play a long up bow D.

mm11. Roll back to the E string and set your Low 1 and Low 2 to play a very-long down bow G followed by a very-long up bow G. Both notes will use the full length of the bow.

mm12. Continue the musical phrase and play a long down bow G. Set your 3rd finger and play a long up bow A. Remove your 3rd finger and play a long down bow Open E. Set your Low 1 and play a long up bow F.

mm13. Hold your Low 1 on the E string while you roll to the A string and set your 3rd finger. Play a very-long down bow D followed by a very-long up bow D. Both notes will use the full length of the bow.

mm14. Set your 3rd finger and play a long down bow D. Remove your 3rd finger and roll to the E string; your Low 1 should still be on the E string. Play a long up bow F. Remove your 1st finger and play a long down bow Open E. Roll to the A string as you quickly set your 1st, Low 2, and 3rd fingers to play a long up bow D.

mm15. Remove your 3rd finger and play a long down bow C. Hop your Low 2 over to the E string as you roll your bow to the E string and play a long up bow G. Hold your Low 2 as you roll back to the A string and cross over your 3rd finger to the A string. Play a long down bow D. Set your 4th finger and play a long up bow E.

mm16. Hop your Low 2 to the A string and play a very-long down bow C followed by a very-long up bow C. Both notes will use the full length of the bow.

J. Offenbach

Figure 7.10
Can-Can

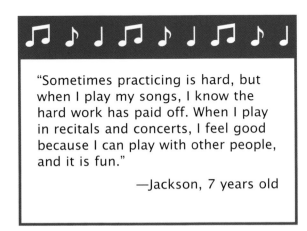

"Sometimes practicing is hard, but when I play my songs, I know the hard work has paid off. When I play in recitals and concerts, I feel good because I can play with other people, and it is fun."

—Jackson, 7 years old

She'll Be Comin' Round the Mountain

Basic song characteristics:

- Metronome: Half note = 96.

- Key signature: C Major, no sharps or flats.

- Time signature: Simple, four beats per measure and the quarter note gets the beat. Half note = 2 beats, quarter note = 1 beat.

- Strings: D string = Low 2 finger pattern, A string = Low 2 finger pattern, E string = Low 1 finger pattern.

- Note names, first line: G, A // C, C, C, C // C, A, G, A // C, E //.

- Rhythm, first line: Very long-very long // long-long-long-long // long-long-long-long // very long-very long //.

- Fingering technical difficulty: To pull back Low 1 F on the E string while the keeping the 3rd finger on the 3rd tape (measure 8). Moving the Low 1 on the E string to a regular 1 on the A string (measure 13). Holding the 3rd third finger G on the D string and placing your 4th finger E on the upper string (measures 14 and 15).

- See the DVD for a performance of the song with the metronome.

Here's how to play the song measure by measure:

mm1. Place your bow near the lower half on the D string and set your 1st, Low 2, and 3rd fingers on the D string. Play a very-long down bow G. Remove your 3rd finger and roll to the A string to play a very-long up bow Open A. Both notes will use the full length of the bow.

mm2. Set your 1st and Low 2 and play four long C's starting down bow.

mm3. Continue the musical phrase and play another long down bow C. Remove all fingers and play a long up bow Open A. Roll to the D string as you cross over your 3rd finger to play a long down bow G. Roll back to the A string and remove all fingers to play a long up bow Open A.

mm4. Set your 1st and Low 2 and play a very-long down bow C. Set your 4th finger on the A string and play a very-long up bow E. Both notes will use the full length of the bow.

mm5. Continue the musical phrase and play another very-long down bow E. Remove your 4th finger and play a long up bow Low 2 C. Set your 3rd finger and play a long down bow D.

mm6. Remove all fingers and roll to the E string. Play four long E's, starting up bow.

mm7.   Quickly set your Low 1 and Low 2 and play a long up bow G. Remove all fingers and play a long down bow Open E. Roll to the A string and set your 1st, Low 2, and 3rd fingers to play a long up bow D. Remove your 3rd finger and play a long down bow C.

mm8.   Set your 3rd finger and play a very-long up bow D. Roll to the E string as you remove all fingers and play a very-long Low 1 F. Both notes will use the full length of the bow.

mm9.   Continue the musical phrase and play a very-long up bow F. Set your Low 2 and play a long down bow G. Remove your 2nd finger and play a long up bow F.

mm10. Remove your Low 1 and play four long Open E's starting down bow.

mm11. Roll to the A string and set your 1st, Low 2, and 3rd finger to play a long down bow D. Remove your 3rd finger and play three long C's starting up bow.

mm12. Remove your 2nd finger and play four long Open A's starting down bow.

mm13. Set your 1st, Low2, and 3rd fingers on the A string and play a long down bow D. Remove your 3rd finger and play a long up bow C. Remove your 2nd finger and play a long down bow B. Remove your 1st finger and play a long up bow Open A.

mm14. Roll to the D string and set your 1st, Low 2, and 3rd fingers to play four long G's starting down bow.

mm15. Hold your 3rd finger on the D string as you roll to the A string and set your 4th finger on the A string. Play a long down bow 4th finger E. Hop your 3rd finger to the A string and play a long up bow 3rd finger D. Remove your 3rd finger and play a long down bow 1st finger B. Hold your 1st finger on the A string as you cross your 3rd finger to the D string. Play a long up bow 3rd finger G.

mm16. Roll back to the A string, set your Low 2 next to your 1st finger, and play a very-long C. Set your 4th finger on the same string and play a very-long up bow E. Both notes will use the full length of the bow.

mm17. Remove your 4th finger and play a very-very-very-long Low 2 C using the full length of the down bow.

Figure 7.11
She'll Be Comin' Round the Mountain

The Blue Danube Waltz

Basic song characteristics:

- Metronome: Quarter note = 80.

- Key signature: C Major, no sharps or flats.

- Time signature: Simple, three beats per measure and the quarter note gets the beat. Dotted half note = 3 beats, half note = 2 beats, quarter note = 1 beat.

- Strings: G string = High 2 finger pattern, D string = Low 2 finger pattern, A string = Low 2 finger pattern, E string = Low 1 finger pattern.

- Note names, first line: C, E, G // G, G // G, E // E, C // C, E, G // G, G // G, F // F, B //.

- Rhythm, first line: Long-long-long // very long-long // very long-long // very long-long // long-long-long // very long-long // very long-long // very long-long //.

- Fingering technical difficulty: To go from a Low 1 F on the E string to a High 2 B on the G string (measures 7, 8, 11, and 12). Going from a High 3 G♯ on the D string to a Low 1 F on the E string (measures 27 and 28).

- Bowing technical difficulty: To stop the bow completely and roll to the next string before playing the next note.

- See the DVD for a performance of the song with the metronome.

Here's how to play the song measure by measure:

mm1. Set your 1st finger on the D string as you place your bow on the G string near the middle of the bow, and cross over your 3rd finger on the G string. Play a long down bow C. Roll to the D string; your 1st finger should be ready to play a long up bow E that is staccato slurred to a long up bow 3rd finger G.

mm2. Play a very-long down bow G. Roll over to the E string and set your Low 1 and Low 2, and play a long up bow G.

mm3. Continue the musical phrase and play a very-long down bow G. Remove all fingers and play a long up bow Open E.

mm4. Continue the musical phrase and play a very-long down bow Open E. Set your 1st finger on the D string as you roll your bow on the G string, and cross over your 3rd finger on the G string. Play a long up bow C.

mm5. Play a long down bow C. Roll to the D string; your 1st finger should be ready to play a long up bow E that is staccato slurred to a long up bow 3rd finger G.

mm6. Play a very-long down bow G. Roll over to the E string and set your Low 1 and Low 2, and play a long up bow G.

mm7. Continue the musical phrase and play a very-long down bow G. Remove your 2nd finger and play a long up bow F.

mm8. Continue the musical phrase and play a very-long down bow F. Roll over to the G string and set your High 2 to play a long up bow B.

mm9. Continue the musical phrase and play another long down bow B. Remove all fingers and roll to the D string to play a long up bow Open D that is slurred to a long up bow Open A.

mm10. Play a very-long down bow Open A. Roll to the E string and set your Low 1, Low 2, and 3rd fingers to play a long up bow A.

mm11. Play a very-long down bow A. Remove your 3rd and 2nd fingers to play a long up bow Low 1 F.

mm12. Continue the musical phrase and play a very-long down bow F. Roll over to the G string and set your High 2 to play a long up bow B.

mm13. Continue the musical phrase and play another long down bow B. Remove all fingers and roll to the D string to play a long up bow Open D that is slurred to a long up bow Open A.

mm14. Play a very-long down bow Open A. Roll to the E string and set your Low 1, Low 2, and 3rd fingers to play a long up bow A.

mm15. Play a very-long down bow A. Remove all fingers to play a long up bow Open E.

mm16. Continue the musical phrase and play a very-long down bow Open E. Set your 1st finger on the D string as you roll your bow on the G string, and cross over your 3rd finger on the G string. Play a long up bow C.

mm17. Play a long down bow C. Roll to the D string; your 1st finger should ready to play a long up bow E that is staccato slurred to a long up bow 3rd finger G.

mm18. Hold your 1st finger on the D string to help you locate the Low 2 on the A string. Roll to the A string and play a very-long down bow C followed by a long up bow C.

mm19. Continue the musical phrase and play another very long down bow C. Hold your 2nd finger on the A string as your cross over your 3rd finger to the D string to play a long up bow G.

mm20. Play a very-long down bow G. Set your 1st finger on the D string as you roll your bow on the G string, and cross over your 3rd finger on the G string. Play a long up bow C.

mm21. Play a long down bow C. Roll to the D string; your 1st finger should ready to play a long up bow E that is staccato slurred to a long up bow 3rd finger G.

mm22. Hold your 1st finger on the D string to help you locate the Low 2 on the A string. Roll to the A string and play a very-long down bow C followed by a long up bow C.

mm23. Continue the musical phrase and play another very-long down bow C. Remove all fingers and play a long up bow Open A.

mm24. Play a very-long down bow Open A. Roll to the D string and play a long up bow Open D.

mm25. Play another long down bow Open D. Roll to the A string, set your 1st and Low 2, and play a long up bow F. Remove all fingers, roll to the A string, and play a long down bow Open A.

mm26. Play a very-very-long Open A, using the full length of the up bow.

mm27. Play a long down bow Open A. Set your 1st finger and play a short up bow B followed by a short down bow Open A at the tip of the bow. Roll to the D string and cross over a stretched High 3 G♯ that will be slurred in a continuous smooth up bow with an Open A.

mm28. Roll to the E string and set your Low 1. Play a very-very-long F, using the full length of your down bow.

mm29. Hold your Low 1 on the E string and cross over a Low 2 on the red tape to the A string. Play a long up bow C. Remove all fingers and play a long down bow Open A. Roll to the D string, set your 1st finger, and play a long up bow E.

mm30. Continue the musical phrase and play a very-long down bow E. Remove your 1st finger and play a long up bow Open D.

mm31. Roll to the A string and play a very-long Open A. Roll to the D string and cross over your 3rd finger to play a long up bow G.

mm32. Hop your 3rd finger to the G string and play a long down bow C. Rest for one beat as you roll to the A string and set your 1st and Low 2, and play a long up bow C.

mm33. Continue the music phrase and play a very-very-long C, using the full length of your down bow.

Strauss

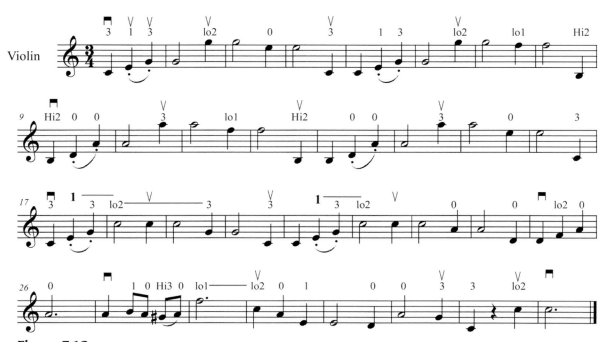

Figure 7.12
The Blue Danube Waltz

The Mexican Hand-Clapping Song

Basic song characteristics:

- Metronome: Quarter note = 96.

- Key signature: C Major, no sharps or flats.

- Time signature: Simple, three beats per measure, and the quarter note gets the beat. Dotted half note = 3 beats, half note = 2 beats, quarter note = 1 beat.

- Strings: A string = Low 2 finger pattern, E string = Low 1 finger pattern.

- Note name, first line: C, C, E // G, E, C // B, rest, A // G // B, B, D // F, D, B // C, rest, A // G //.

- Rhythm, first line: Long-long-long // long-long-long // long-quarter rest-long // very very long // long-long-long // long-long-long // long-quarter rest-long // very very long //.

- Fingering technical difficulty: To move from a regular 1 B on the A string to a Low 1 F on the E string, and then back to a regular 1 on the A string (measures 5, 6, 13, and 14).

- See the DVD for a performance of the song with the metronome.

Here's how to play the song measure by measure:

mm1. Place your bow near the lower half on the A string, and set down your 1st and Low 2. Play two long C's, starting down bow. Roll to the E string and play a long down bow Open E.

mm2. Set your 1st and Low 2 on the E string and play a long up bow G. Remove all fingers, and play a long down bow Open E. Roll to the A string, set your 1st and Low 2, and play a long up bow C.

mm3. Remove your 2nd finger and play a long down bow B. Hold your 1st finger while you rest for one beat and roll to the E string to set your Low 2 and 3rd finger. Play a long up bow A.

mm4. Remove your 3rd finger and play a very-very-long Low 2 G, using the full length of the down bow.

mm5. Roll to the A string; your 1st finger should still be on 1st tape. Play two long B's, starting up bow. Set your 3rd finger and play a long up bow D.

mm6. Hold your 3rd finger on the A string, while you roll to the E string and pull back your Low 1 to play a long down bow F. Roll back to the A string, and play the holding 3rd finger D with a long up bow. Hop your 1st finger to the A string on 1st tape, and remove your 3rd finger to play a long down bow B.

mm7. Set your Low 2, and play a long up bow C. Rest for one beat as you hop your Low 2 to the E string and set your 3rd finger to play a long down bow A.

mm8. Remove your 3rd finger, and play a very-very-long G, using the full length of your up bow.

mm9. Roll to the A string and set down your 1st and Low 2. Play two long C's, starting down bow. Roll to the E string and play a long down bow Open E.

mm10. Set your 1st and Low 2 on the E string and play a long up bow G. Remove all fingers and play a long down bow Open E. Roll to the A string, set your 1st and Low 2, and play a long up bow C.

mm11. Remove your 2nd finger and play a long down bow B. Hold your 1st finger while you rest for one beat and roll to the E string to set your Low 2 and 3rd fingers. Play a long up bow A.

mm12. Remove your 3rd finger and play a very-very-long Low 2 G, using the full length of the down bow.

mm13. Roll to the A string; your 1st finger should still be on the 1st tape. Play two long B's, starting up bow. Set your 3rd finger and play a long up bow D.

mm14. Hold your 3rd finger on the A string while you roll to the E string and pull back your Low 1 to play a long down bow F. Roll back to the A string and play the holding 3rd finger D with a long up bow. Hop your 1st finger to the A string on 1st tape and remove your 3rd finger to play a long down bow B.

mm15. Set your Low 2 and play a long up bow C. Rest for one beat as you remove your 2nd finger to play a long down bow B.

mm16. Set your 2nd finger again and play a very-very-long C, using the full length of the up bow.

mm17. Roll to the E string and set your Low 1, Low 2, and 3rd fingers to play a very-very-long A using the full length of the down bow.

mm18. Play another very-very-long A, using the full length of the up bow.

mm19. Play two long A's, starting down bow. Remove your 3rd and Low 2 to play a long down bow F.

mm20. Set your 3rd finger again and play a long up bow A. Remove your 3rd finger and play two long F's, starting down bow.

mm21. Set your Low 2 and play a very-very-long G, using the full length of the down bow.

mm22. Play another very-very-long G, using the full length of the up bow.

mm23. Play two long G's, starting down bow. Remove all fingers and play the Open E with a long down bow.

mm24. Set your Low 2 again and play a long up bow G. Remove your Low 2 and play two long Open E's, starting down bow.

mm25. Set your Low 1 and play a very-very-long F, using the full length of your down bow.

mm26. Play another very-very-long F, using the full length of your up bow.

mm27. Play two long F's, starting down bow. Hold your 1st finger on the E string as you roll to the A string and cross over your 3rd finger to play a long down bow D.

mm28. Remove your 3rd finger as you roll to your Low 1 on the E string and play a long up bow F. Set your Low 2 and play a long down bow G. Remove your 2nd finger and play a long up bow F.

mm29. Remove your 1st finger and play a very-long down bow E. Set your Low 1, Low 2, and 3rd finger to play a long up bow A.

mm30. Remove your 3rd finger and play a very-very-long G, using the full length of your down bow.

mm31. Remove all fingers and play a long up bow Open E. Roll to the A string and quickly set your 1st and Low 2, and play a long down bow C. Set your 3rd finger and play a long up bow D.

mm32. Roll to the E string, and play a long down bow Open E. Set your Low 1 and play a long up bow F that is staccato slurred to a long up bow G.

mm33. Set your 3rd finger and play a very-very-long A using the full length of the down bow.

mm34. Play another very-very-long A, using the full length of the up bow.

mm35. Play two long A's, starting down bow. Remove your 3rd and Low 2 to play a long down bow F.

mm36. Set your 3rd finger again and play a long up bow A. Remove your 3rd finger and play two long F's, starting down bow.

mm37. Set your Low 2 and play a very-very-long G, using the full length of the down bow.

mm38. Play another very-very-long G, using the full length of the up bow.

mm39. Play two long G's, starting down bow. Remove all fingers and play the Open E with a long down bow.

mm40. Set your Low 2 again and play a long up bow G. Remove your Low 2 and play two long Open E's, starting down bow.

mm41. Set your Low 1 and play a very-very-long F, using the full length of your down bow.

mm42. Play another very-very-long F, using the full length of your up bow.

mm43. Play two long F's, starting down bow. Hold your 1st finger on the E string as you roll to the A string and cross over your 3rd finger to play a long down bow D.

mm44. Remove your 3rd finger as you roll to your Low 1 on the E string and play a long up bow F. Set your Low 2 and play a long down bow G. Remove your 2nd finger, and play a long up bow F.

mm45. Remove your 1st finger and play two long Open E's, starting down bow. Set your Low 1 and play a long down bow F.

mm46. Set your Low 2 and play a long up bow G. Rest for one beat as your roll to the A string and set your 1st finger on the tape to play a long down bow B.

mm47. Set your Low 2 and play a very-long up bow C. Set your 3rd finger and play a long down bow D.

mm48. Remove your 3rd finger and play a very-very-long C, using the full length of your up bow.

Folk Song

Figure 7.13
The Mexican hand-clapping song

A

GIUSEPPE TARTINI

L'ISTRIA

History of the
Violin

N OW PICTURE YOURSELF AS THE newest member, associating with one of the most prestigious and celebrated lineages of your time, the lineage of music, by studying the beautiful and skillful art of the violin. This lineage predates the 1600s and is recorded over time from masterpiece to masterpiece of each composer to the present day. This chapter will guide you through a discovery of how each century affected music and how music affected each society, and will list the major composers for violin in works such as violin concertos, chamber music, and symphonic and operatic literature.

Origination of the Violin

P RIOR TO THE 1600S, THE FRENCH troubadours fostered a popular demand for professional traveling entertainers, like the jongleurs and minstrels, to perform songs of dance using the ancestors of the violin for their penetrating tone and lively rhythmic articulation. These minstrels became very important in court life, which increased the musician's social status.

Here's a timeline of evolution for the violin:

- *Rebec, 1300-1700*—Even though it has no relation to the violin, this instrument was pear-shaped with a neck and peg box. There were no soundpost or frets, and the three strings were tuned in fifths. It had a small, nasal tone quality, and the bow was held overhand. It later evolved into the kit (1550-1800).

Figure 7.1
Rebec and bow

- *Renaissance fiddle, 1500*—An ancestor of the violin, this instrument had five strings and frets. Shaped like the violin, it had a separate neck and fingerboard, and the top and back were connected with ribs.

- *Lira Da Braccia, 1500*—Closely resembles the violin outline with an arched back and top, overlapping edges, ribs, soundpost, F-holes, and an hourglass figure or bouts that made it easy to bow the seven strings, two of which were drones, or constant resonating strings.

Figure 7.2
Lira

- *Violin, 1550*—The true four-string violin, created in Northern Italy by Giovan Giacoba dalla Corna and Zanetto de Michelis da Montichiaro. Later it was perfected by the Amati family of Cremona.

There are three main influences that helped the violin to evolve over time:

- *Craftsmen*—Adjusting the shape and acoustics of the violin to meet the constant demands of the violinists and composers.

- *Violinists*—Discovering new agility, speed, and special techniques, while exploring the full note range of a violin.

- *Composers*—Progressing the melody line and pushing the technical ability of the violinist.

Here's the family tree of the great violin makers:

- *Amati Family, 1555-1740*—Antonio Amati (1555-1640) founded the School of Cremona with Girolamo Amati (1556-1630). Nicola Amati, Girolamo's son, continued the legacy by teaching many of the other famous violin makers of that time.

- *Antonio Stradivarius, 1644-1737*—Over his lifetime, he produced around 1,000 instruments. His designs are regarded as the finest achievement of the school of Cremona, creating the *Stradivarius Violin Model,* which all other successors emulate.

Figure 7.4
Stradivarius violin

Figure 7.3
An Amati violin

✎ *Guarneri Family, 1626-1744*—Andrea Guarneri (1626-1698), as a pupil of Nicola Amati of the School of Cremona, forged the way for Giuseppe G.B. Guarneri (1666-1739) and the famous son Giuseppe "del Gesu" Guarneri (1698-1744). "Del Gesu" created around 200 violins in his lifetime. These violins rivaled the models of Stradivarius in terms of volume and power due to the larger size of the Guarneri violin, made famous by the violinist Niccolò Paganini.

✎ *Jacob Stainer, 1621-1683*—The Northern Alps violin maker whose violins surpassed those of the School of Cremona in the hands of famous violinist by the names of J.S. Bach, F. Veracini, and L. Mozart. Regrettably, with no successors, the Stainer label ended with Jacob Stainer.

Figure 7.6
A Stainer violin

Figure 7.5
A Guarneri violin

Famous Composers Who Were Violinists

OVER THE CENTURIES, magnificent violin literature has been created by some of the most influential composers of the time. Many of these composers were violinists themselves. This section lists, in chronological order, some of the most famous composers who have touched our hearts with their compositional masterpieces for the violin.

- *Arcangelo Corelli, 1653-1713*—An Italian composer and violinist whose violin sonatas (three or more movements), chamber music (small group of instruments), and the first forms of concerto grosso (music passed between a small group of soloist and a full orchestra) changed the playing technique on the violin for the 18th and 19th centuries.

- *Antonio Vivaldi, 1678-1741*—An ordained priest in Vienna who established the "lively-slow-lively" sections of the ternary format of a concerto (one solo instrument is accompanied by an orchestra), and added the first cadenza (a solo to demonstrate the true virtuosity of a violinist).

Figure 7.7
Arcangelo Corelli

Figure 7.8
Antonio Vivaldi

❧ *Johann-Sebastian Bach, 1685-1750—* Most famous for his work in Leipzig, he composed over 200 cantatas (vocal compositions with an instrumental accompaniment), multiple passions (music set to Biblical text), motets (religious vocal music), masses (religious instrumental music), chorals, works for the harpsichord, and the famous sonatas and partitas (dance-based movements) for the violin.

Figure 7.9
Johann-Sebastian Bach

❧ *Giuseppe Tartini, 1692-1770—*During his musical career, he composed close to150 concertos and 100 sonatas for the violin, the most famous being *The Devil's Trill.*

Figure 7.10
Giuseppe Tartini

❧ *Wolfgang Amadeus Mozart, 1756-1791—* Even though he lived a short life, he left behind a famous legacy of over 600 brilliant musical compositions that poured from the creativity of his heart, mind, and soul. He composed in all aspects through a variety genre with ingenuity, including five violin concertos that remain among the most popular violin concertos to date.

Figure 7.11
Wolfgang Amadeus Mozart

- *Niccolò Paganini, 1782-1840*—Undoubtedly the greatest talent on violin that ever existed. He had an unprecedented skill, technique, and fearlessness for pushing the physical limits of the violin and violinist. He composed many works for the violin, including the 24 caprices.

Figure 7.12
Niccolò Paganini

- *Felix Mendelssohn, 1809-1847*—A child prodigy, he started performing his own works in public prior to 12 years of age. His violin concerto ranks among the most famous of all violin concertos to date.

Figure 7.13
Felix Mendelssohn

- *Henryk Wieniawski, 1835-1880*—Studied at the Paris Conservatory and was considered to be a genius on violin. He composed some of the most significant works in the violin repertoire. His two violin concertos, the second concerto in D minor and the celebrated *Scherzo Tarantelle*, are very popular for their Slavic flavor and virtuosity on the violin.

Figure 7.14
Henryk Wieniawski

- *Pablo de Sarasate, 1844-1908*—Studied at the Paris Conservatory, and then dedicated the greater part of his career to tours in Europe, America, and Asia. His compositions are largely flamboyant showpieces intended to display his considerable technique. His best known works are *Zigeunerweisen* and the *Carmen Fantasy* violin concertos, which are composed of popular Bohemian and gypsy melodies.

Figure 7.15
Pablo de Sarasate

Famous Composers and Their Times

OVER THE CENTURIES, MUSIC HAS greatly influenced society through inspiration and creativity, and society has greatly influenced music through education, religion, and technology. Each century is unique in regards to the evolution of the delicate balance between the effects that music and society have on advancing the human race. As the newest member of this prestigious linage, it is important to know your roots. In this section, you will discover the events that took place in each century that directly influenced the delicate balance between music and society, and how the major composers reflected society through their works of art.

The Medieval Period and the Renaissance: 12th to 16th Centuries

The Middle Ages saw constant change in religion, hierarchies, kingdoms, and nations. Universities were born through the cathedral schools, giving rise to non-religious literature such as Chaucer's *Canterbury Tales,* and to artists such as Leonardo da Vinci and Michelangelo. Music underwent many changes from the sacred plain chant of the monasteries to secular songs of the troubadours entertaining from village to village.

Here are the major composers of the time and their popular works:

- *Hildegard of Bingen, 1098-1179—* Sequences (repeating musical patterns) and hymns (religious songs).

- *Guillaume de Machaut, 1160-1225—* Mass of Our Lady, a polyphonic (two or more independent melodic voices) mass.

- *Guillaume Dufay, 1400-1474—*Sacred (religious) and secular (non-religious) vocal works.

- *Carlo Gesualdo, 1561-1613—*Madrigals (non-religious texts set to two or more voices).

- *Andrea Gabrieli, 1510-1586—*Sacred choral and instrumental works.

The Baroque Era: 17th to Mid-18th Century

The Baroque era was formed on the back of the 30-year war between the Catholics and the Protestants. From this political revolution came an abundant advancement of technology, literature, art, and music. This era developed the brilliant minds of Kepler, Galileo, Newton, Shakespeare, Moliere, and Racine, and resulted in the sculptures and paintings of Bernini, Caravaggio, and Rembrandt. In music, the opera (dramatic work for voice), oratorio (large musical composition including an orchestra, a choir, and soloists), cantata, and sonata were born, and Baroque music reached its pinnacle through the genius melodic writings of Bach and Handel.

Here are the major composers of the time and their popular works:

- *Claudio Monteverdi, 1567-1643—The Legend of Orpheus*, the first true Italian opera.

- *Jean-Baptiste Lully, 1632-1687—Armide, Tragedies Lyriques*, French opera.

- *Johann Pachelbel, 1653-1706—Canon in D, Magnificat in D.*

- *Henry Purcell, 1659-1695—Dido and Aeneas*, opera.

- *Arcangelo Corelli, 1653-1713—Concerti Grossi, Op.6, 'La follia'* violin sonata in D minor.

- *Antonio Vivaldi, 1678-1741—The Four Seasons, Gloria in D.*

- *Johann Sebastian Bach, 1685-1750—Brandenburg Concertos, St. Matthew Passion*, sonatas and partitas for violin, *The Well-Tempered Clavier.*

- *George Frideric Handel, 1685-1759—Messiah, Water Music.*

- *Georg Philipp Teleman, 1681-1767—*Violin concertos, Tafelmusik (background music for feasts, banquets, and other outdoor events).

The Classical Era: Mid-18th to Mid-19th Century

The Classical era was the age of reason, where society, music, and architecture dramatically changed due to the Age of Enlightenment, the American Revolution, the French Revolution, and Classicism. In music, the orchestra flourished past the confines of the opera and developed into a self-sustaining art form, giving rise to the symphony (large composition, usually four movements in length) and the concerto (one solo instrument accompanied by an orchestra) compositions.

Here are the major composers of the time and their popular works:

- *Christoph Gluck, 1714-1787—Orpheus and Eurydice, Alceste*, opera.

- *Franz Joseph Haydn, 1732-1809—*"The father of the symphony" composed over 100 symphonies including the *Surprise Symphony in G* and the *London Symphony in D.*

- *Luigi Boccherini, 1743-1805—Symphonies in D minor*, string quartets.

- *Wolfgang Amadeus Mozart, 1756-1791—*Established the modern form of the concert, and is known for *Symphony No.41 Jupiter, Requiem in D Minor*, and violin concertos.

- *Franz Schubert, 1797-1828—The Great Symphony No.9, Die Winterreise.*

The Romantic Era: 19th Century

The industrial revolution formed a rapidly growing urban and middle-class population, and for the first time, composers earned a significant income from their work in the form of printed sheet music. On a larger scale, music societies, now freed from aristocratic control, sponsored public orchestral concerts as a feature of city life throughout Europe and the United States.

Here are the major composers of the time and their popular works:

- *Ludwig van Beethoven, 1770-1827—Choral Symphony No.9, Eroica* and pastoral symphonies.

- *Niccolò Paganini, 1782-1840—24* caprices for violin, violin concertos.

- *Felix Mendelssohn, 1809-1847—Symphony No.4 Italian, Midsummer Night's Dream,* violin concerto.

- *Hector Berlioz, 1803-1869—Symphonie Fantastique, Op.14.*

- *Charles Gounod, 1818-1893—*The opera *Faust.*

- *Frederic Chopin, 1810-1849—*Piano concertos and sonatas.

- *Robert Schumann, 1810-1856—*Piano concertos, violin concertos, symphonies no.1-4.

- *Franz Liszt, 1811-1886—*Piano sonata in B Minor, Hungarian rhapsodies.

- *Giuseppe Verdi, 1813-1901—*The operas—*Otello, Rigoletto, La Traviata.*

- *Richard Wagner, 1813-1883—*The operas—*Tristan und Isolde, The Ring.*

- *Edouard Lalo, 1823-1892—Symphonie Espagnole* violin concerto.

- *Johann Strauss II 1825-1899—*Waltzes and other dances.

- *Camille Saint-Saens, 1835-1921—The Carnival of the Animals, Danse Macabre, Symphony No.3, Introduction and Rondo Capriccioso* violin concerto.

- *Georges Bizet, 1838-1875—*The opera *Carmen.*

- *Johannes Brahms, 1833-1897—*Symphonies and violin concertos.

- *Nikolai Rimsky-Korsakov, 1844-1908—Sheherazade, Capriccio Espagnol.*

- *Pyotr llyich Tchaikovsky, 1840-1893—Pathetique symphony no. 6 in B minor, Sleeping Beauty, The Nutcracker, Romeo and Juliet,* violin concertos.

- *Antonin Dvorak, 1841-1904—The New World Symphony No.9,* violin concerto, Slavonic dances.

- *Giacomo Puccini, 1858-1924—*The operas—*Tosca, La Boheme, Madame Butterfly.*

- *Gustav Mahler, 1860-1911—Symphony No.9, Songs of a Wayfarer.*

- *Claude Debussy, 1862-1918—La Mer,* prelude to afternoon of a faun.

- *Richard Strauss, 1864-1949—Don Juan, Don Quixote, Elektra, Metamorphosen.*

- *Jean Sibelius, 1865-1957—Symphony No.5, Violin Concerto in D Minor, Op.47, Finlandia.*

- *Maurice Ravel, 1875-1937—Bolero, Rapsodie Espagnole, Daphnis et Chloe.*

The 20th Century

Orchestra and opera concerts remain the main focus in classical music, while major technological developments in broadcasting, accelerated by World War I, transformed the musical era. Recording systems like Edison's cylinder phonograph in 1877, disc and magnetic tape in 1920, Columbia Records' long-playing disc in 1948, stereophonic reproduction in 1957, Philips' compact cassette in 1963, and the early arrival of digital recording and compact discs in the early 1980s, helped catapult musical performances and their composers into a new level of recognition in today's society. Today, a composer or musician can be employed by a wide number of patronages from government, universities, recording companies, film soundtracks, musical organizations, symphonies, and as always, the Church.

Here are the major composers of the time and their popular works:

- *Sergi Rachmaninov, 1873-1943—Piano Concerto No.2, Symphony No.2 and No.3.*

- *Gustav Holst, 1874-1934—The Planets.*

- *Charles Ives, 1874-1954—Symphony No.3,* string quartet.

- *Ottorino Respighi, 1879-1936—Pines of Rome, Fountains of Rome.*

- *Bela Bartok, 1881-1945—Concerto for Orchestra, Violin Concerto No.2.*

- *Igor Stravinsky, 1882-1971—The Rite of Spring, Petrushka, Firebird.*

- *Alban Berg, 1885-1935—*Violin concerto.

- *Sergei Prokofiev, 1891-1953—Peter and the Wolf, Violin Concerto No.1.*

- *Paul Hindemith, 1895-1963—Symphonic Metamorphosis.*

- *George Gershwin, 1898-1937—Rhapsody in Blue, Porgy and Bess, An American in Paris.*

- *Aaron Copland, 1900-1990— Appalachian Spring, Billy the Kid, Rodeo.*

- *Dmitri Shostakovich, 1906-1975— Symphony No.10, No.1, and No.4.*

- *Samuel Barber, 1910-1981—Adagio for Strings,* violin concerto.

- *John Cage, 1912-1992—Concerto for Piano and Orchestra, Three Dances for Prepared Piano.*

- *Benjamin Britten, 1913-1976—Peter Grimes, War Requiem.*

- *Leonard Bernstein, 1918-1990—West Side Story, Candide.*

Many people think that composing is a lost art, and that the era of composing ended with Mozart and Bach. In fact, composing is alive and well today, but instead of composing for the king in court, most of the masterpieces of modern composers are performed for the ticket holder. From Luke Skywalker's triumph over the Death Star to classic melodies of *The Godfather*, modern composers like Nino Rota, Basil Poledouris, John Williams, Bernard Herrmann, Jerry Goldsmith, James Horner, Alan Silvestri, John Debney, Howard Shoremake, and more, make movies come to life with emotion, suspense, and excitement.

Continue the
Journey

PICTURE YOURSELF CONTINUING your journey
through the world of music by developing the necessary
skills to become an intermediate violinist, and then sharp-
ening those skills and learning increasingly difficult techniques
and nuances on your way to becoming an advanced violinist.
Your dream might be to become a member of an orchestra,
start a string quartet, join a jazz or rock band, go on tour with
a Broadway show, perform in movie soundtracks, teach others
how to play violin, or simply enjoy playing the violin as a
rewarding hobby. Remember, anything is possible!

Where to Go from Here

THE NEXT STEP IN YOUR musical journey is to continue your education by increasing your knowledge of techniques and repertoire for the violin. To truly master the art of playing violin is a life-long journey, one that is filled with meaning and purpose, and driven by gratifying achievement and the excitement of new discoveries. These new discoveries can be facilitated through the use of technique books, mastering violin solos, online learning tools, and through one-on-one training in private lessons.

Here's a list of technique books that every violinist should study:

- *Wohlfahrt, Foundation Studies for the Violin, Book 1, Carl Fischer edition*—This book will teach you how to utilize all aspects of your bow through easy-to-read song exercises.

- *Introducing the Positions for Violin Volumes 1 and 2 by Harvey Whistler, Rubank edition*—These books will teach you how to shift and play in every position through easy-to-read song exercises.

- *Melodious Double-Stops for Violin by Josephine Trott, book 1, Schirmer's edition*—This book will teach you how to play two or more notes at the same time, fiddle style, using fun and challenging songs.

- *Sevcik, School of Violin Technique, Part 1, Exercises in the first position, Schirmer's edition*—This book will teach your left hand speed and accuracy through specific repeating patterns, similar to a challenging word puzzle for your fingers.

- *Mazas, seventy-five melodious and progressive studies, book 1, Schirmer's edition*—This book will transition you into an advanced performer through beautifully written melodies covering all shifting positions and bowing styles.

To help develop your musical repertoire, I suggest the following books on violin solos for self-starters or disciplined students:

- *Suzuki Books 1–6*—These books represent the most popular violin repertoire presented in an easy-to-learn format. Each new song and book is a steady progression of learning through violin sheet music and CDs.

- *CD, Leila Josefowicz, Bohemian Rhapsodies*—The individual violin concertos on this CD are the *Carmen Fantasy* by Sarasate, *Introductions and Rondo Capriccioso* by Saint-Saens, *Zigeunerweisen* by Sarasate, *Polonaise No. 1* by Wieniawski, *Meditation de Thais* by Massenet, *Tzigane* by Ravel, and *Poeme* by Chausson.

- CD, Leila Josefowicz, violin concertos—The individual violin concertos on this CD are the *Concerto in E Minor* by Mendelssohn, *Valse-Scherzo* by Tchaikovsky, and *Concerto in A Minor* by Glazunov.

- CD, Anne-Sophie Mutter, violin concerto—*Concerto* for violin and *Orchestra in D minor* by Sibelius.

- CD, Rachel Podger, Sonatas and Partitas Vol.1 and 2—Bach's *6 Sonatas and Partitas* for violin.

- CD, Isaac Stern, violin concertos—Mozart's violin concertos.

Here's a list of online learning tools for students who need more guidance:

- www.VideoViolinLessons.com—The Academy of Music Performance's violin lessons on DVD include a beginner series that covers all the songs covered in the *Picture Yourself Playing Violin* book, an intermediate series that covers Suzuki books 2 and 3, a holiday series that covers all-time favorite holiday carols with an accompaniment CD, and the master class series that covers most of the violin repertoire.

- www.violinmasterclass.com—Provides extra picture and video references for learning bow and fingering techniques on the violin.

Here are few tips when selecting a private violin instructor, for those who need one-on-one mentoring:

- Consider how proficient you want to become on the violin and with which pace you would like to learn new skills and techniques. Decide if you want to focus on learning fun songs or if you want to master the more technical aspects of the violin. Some teachers are very strict and while others are very relaxed when it comes to teaching violin.

- Inquire at a local music store or high school for references on a violin instructor, and be sure to ask about professional qualifications and background when interviewing a potential instructor.

- To finalize your selection, study with the instructor over a trial period of a few lessons so that you can evaluate the teaching style and personality of the instructor. Choose someone who can inspire you to practice, and to whom you feel comfortable expressing your ideas and questions about the violin.

- Take into consideration your budget, and if the instructor charges per lesson, per month, or if there is a payment contract you will be obligated to uphold.

"Bach once said, 'There's nothing remarkable about it. All one has to do is hit the right keys at the right time and the instrument plays itself.' Good luck to you as you begin your musical journey."

—Chen, 15 years old

Final Thoughts from Mrs. Seidel

CONGRATULATIONS! You should be very proud of all that you have accomplished reading this book. Hopefully this book and its DVD companion have transformed you from a true beginner into a budding violinist. You now have the knowledge of how to create rich warm tones, and the experience of how to read sheet music while performing on the violin with proper bowing and fingering techniques and specialty sound effects.

I encourage you to show off your new-found skills on the violin to your friends and family, and to find a group of musicians with which to practice your new craft. Have fun when you play, and remember not to just practice notes, but to enjoy the beauty of the violin by creating music!

It is my sincere hope that this book has guided you through your first steps in learning to play the violin, and instilled in you a desire to continue your musical education.

Remember to keep your fingers round and your wrist down, and hopefully I will see your next lesson.

—Mrs. Seidel

Index

A

accelerando, 89

accents, 104

accessories, 6–7

accidentals, 83

adjusting

    bridge, 27

    shoulder rest, 20

Amati family, 156, 157

anticipating

    grace notes, 92

    string changes, 56

applying fingering tapes, 48–49

arch of the bridge, 11

arm movement, bowing, 39–40

articulation, slurs, 99

assignment of notes to strings, 72–73

A string note names, 72

attaching

    shoulder rest, 20–23

    sponge, 21

auto-chromatic tuners, 25

B

Ba Ba Black Sheep, 115–116

Baccherini, Luigi, 163

Bach, Johann-Sebastian, 158, 160, 163

back side of violin, 12

ball E string, 16

Barber, Samuel, 165

bar line, 75

Baroque era, composers of, 162–163

Bartok, Bela, 165

bass bar, 10

beat note rhythm exercise, 86

beats per measure, 84–85

Beethoven, Ludwig von, 164

Berlioz, Hector, 164

Bernstein, Leonard, 165

Bizet, Georges, 164

Blue Danube Waltz, The, 147–149

body posture, 22

    holding the violin, 1, 20–23

    tuning the violin, 25

books, reference, 168–169

bounce, fingers, 53

bouncing bow, 42

bow, 7

    holding, 2

    notes, 2

    pinch hold, 105

    placement, 103

    preparing, 14

    rebec and, 156

    roll the, 38

    selecting, 13–15

    square zone, 102

bowing techniques, 29

    arm movement, 39–40

    commanding strokes, 104–106

    direction, 41

    divisions and rhythms, 43–44

    pencil hold, 30–31

    placement optimization, 34–36

    right hand finger exercises, 32–33

    short strokes, 102–104

    smooth strokes, 101–102

    sound effects, 107–108

    specialties, 101–108

    speed and pressure, 42

    string rolls, 37–38

    weight distribution of the bow, 41–43

boxed rosin, 7

Brahms, Johannes, 164

bridge, 6, 10–11

    adjusting, 27

    metal practice mute, 18

Britten, Benjamin, 165

C

Cage, John, 165

Can-Can, 141–143

cases, selecting, 6, 7

changing strings, 58

charts

    High 2 finger pattern, 58

    High 3 finger pattern, 60

    Low 1 finger pattern, 60

    Low 2 finger pattern, 59

    notes, 57

    rhythm, 85

Chopin, Frederic, 164

chromatic fingering, 98

Circle of 5th, 79

Classical era, composers of, 163

"Claw Side to Side Extensions" exercise, 33

"Claw Up and Straight Down" exercise, 32

close elbow arm position, 40

collegno, 107

combinations, fingering techniques, 98–99

commanding strokes, 104–106

components

    of the bow, 13

    of violin outfits, 6–7

composers, 75

    Baccherini, Luigi, 163

    Bach, Johann-Sebastian, 158, 160, 163

    Barber, Samuel, 165

    Baroque era, 162–163

    Bartok, Bela, 165

    Beethoven, Ludwig von, 164

    Berlioz, Hector, 164

    Bernstein, Leonard, 165

    Bizet, Georges, 164

    Brahms, Johannes, 164

    Britten, Benjamin, 165

    Cage, John, 165

    Chopin, Frederic, 164

    Classical era, 163

Copland, Aaron, 165
Corelli, Arcangelo, 159, 163
Debussy, Claude, 164
de Darasate, Pablo, 161
de Machaut, Guillaume, 162
Dufay, Guiliaume, 162
Dvorak, Antonin, 164
Gershwin, George, 165
Gluck, Christoph, 163
Gounod, Charles, 164
Handel, George Frideric, 163
Haydn, Franz Joseph, 163
Hildegard of Bingen, 162
Hindemith, Paul, 165
Holst, Gustav, 165
influence on violin design, 157
Ives, Charles, 165
Lalo, Edouard, 164
Liszt, Franz, 164
Lully, Jean-Baptiste, 163
Mahler, Gustav, 164
Medieval period, 162
Mendelssohn, Felix, 161, 164
Monteverdi, Claudia, 163
Mozart, Wolfgang Amadeus, 160, 163
Pachelbet, Johann, 163
Paganini, Niccolò, 161, 164
Prokofiev, Sergei, 165
Puccini, Giacomo, 164
Purcell, Henry, 163
Rachmaninov, Sergi, 165
Ravel, Maurice, 164
Renaissance period, 162

Respighi, Ottorino, 165
Rimsky-Karsakov, Nikalai, 164
Romantic era, 164
Saint-Saens, Camille, 164
Schubert, Franz, 163
Schumann, Robert, 164
Shostakovich, Dmitri, 165
Sibelius, Jean, 164
Strauss, Richard, 164
Strauss II, Johann, 164
Stravinsky, Igor, 165
Tartini, Guiseppe, 160
Tchaikovsky, Pyotr, 164
Teleman, Georg Philipp, 163
20th century, 165
Verdi, Guiseppe, 164
Vivaldi, Antonio, 159, 163
Wagner, Richard, 164
who were violinists, 159–161
Wieniawski, Henryk, 161
compound time, 84
Copland, Aaron, 165
Corelli, Arcangelo, 159, 163
Corna, Giovan Giacoba dalla, 156
counting vibrato hits, 100
craftsman, influence of violin design, 157
Cremona, Amati family of, 156, 157
crescendo, 109–110
cross back arm position, 39
cross over and hop position, 54–55
cross over arm position, 39
crunchy tone, 42

D

Debussy, Claude, 164
decrescendo, 110
de Darasate, Pablo, 161
de Machaut, Guillaume, 162
detache, 101–102
direction, bowing, 41
divisions
    of beat exercise, 86
    bow, 43–44
dotted rhythms exercise, 87–88
double bar lines, 75
double stops, 98–99
D string note names, 73
Dufay, Guiliaume, 162
Dvorak, Antonin, 164
dynamics, 109
    special effects with, 109–111

E

elbows, swing, 55–56
electronic tuners, 18
endings, 75
equalizing weight of the bow, 41
E string
    fine tuners, 12
    loop or ball, selecting, 16
    note names, 72
Evah Pirazzi strings, 16
exercises. *See also* practice
    beat note rhythm, 86
    divisions of beat, 86

dotted rhythms, 87–88
finger patterns, 59
finger-pattern slurs, 62–64
High 2 finger pattern, 58
holding beats, 87
mixtures, 88
reading note names, 75
rhythm, 44, 85–88
right hand finger
    "Claw Side to Side Extensions," 33
    "Claw Up and Straight Down," 32
scales, playing, 80–82
vibrato, 99–100
extensions, fingers, 96–97

F

false harmonics, 95–96
fermata, 89
F-holes, 6
    height of the bridge, 11
fiddle, Renaissance, 156
fifths, 61
fine tuners, 6, 12
    strings, tuning, 25
fingerboard, 6
fingering techniques, 47
    combinations, 98–99
    fingers, moving, 53–56
    hand, setting the, 50–53
    musical ABCs, 57
    patterns, 58–60
    pattern slurs, 62–64

reading straight across, 61

signs, 95

specialties, 92–100

tapes, applying, 48–49, 80

finger rock vibrato, 100

fingers. *See also* **fingering techniques**

bounce, 53

cross over and hop, 54–55

extensions, 96–97

notes, 1

pattern slurs, 62–64

right hand finger exercises, 32–33

spacing, 31

strike, 54

touching, 94

first ending, 75

1st–4th fingers on strings, 76

five-step practice method, 114

flat notes, 57

order of, 78–79

flat pitch, 25

flat scales, 82

forzando (Fz), 111

four long note rhythm exercise, 44

four peg fine tuners, 12

G

Gabrieli, Andrea, 162

gauge, selecting strings, 17

Gershwin, George, 165

Gesualdo, Carlo, 162

glazy tone, 42

glissando, 97–98

Gluck, Christoph, 163

Go Tell Aunt Rhody, **121–122**

Gounod, Charles, 164

grace note, 92–93

G string note names, 73

Guarneri family, 158

H

hair, bow, 14. *See also* **bow**

half step chromatic glissando, 97

Hamilton two-section music stand, 19

hand, setting the, 50–53

Handel, George Frideric, 163

harmonics, 95–96

glissandos, 98

Haydn, Franz Joseph, 163

heavy varnish, 9

height of the bridge, 11

High 2 finger pattern, 58

High 3 finger pattern, 60

Hildegard of Bingen, 162

Hindemith, Paul, 165

history of violin, 155–165

holding

beats exercise, 87

the bow, 2

pencil hold, 30–31

the violin, 1, 20–23, 50

Holst, Gustav, 165

Hot Cross Buns, **2**

I

index finger, bow placement of, 35
instructors, selecting, 169
intervals, 76
invisible track, 40
Ives, Charles, 165

K

key change, 83
key signatures, 75, 78–83
    flats, finding, 79–80
    names, 79
    sharps, finding, 79
    specialties, 83
    trilling, 93
Kun original shoulder rest, 17
    adjusting, 20

L

Lalo, Edouard, 164
leaning bridges, 27
ledger lines, 70–71
left hand, bow placement of, 35
left pizzicato, 96
legato, 101
lessons, 169
lifts, up-bow, 105
Lightly Row, 117–118
lines
    bar line, 75
    double bar lines, 75
    ledger, 70–71
    notes, 68–69
lira, 156
Liszt, Franz, 164
location of finger tape placement, 48
long-tip-tip-long-frog-frog rhythm exercise, 44
loop E string, 16
Low 1 finger pattern, 60
Low 2 finger pattern, 59
Lully, Jean-Baptiste, 163

M

Mahler, Gustav, 164
maintenance
    rosin, applying to bow, 14
    strings, replacing, 26–27
Manhasset Tall Symphony music stand, 19
marking finger tape placement, 48
martale, 106
measure, beats per, 84–85
Medieval period, composers of, 162
Mendelssohn, Felix, 161, 164
mentoring, one-on-one, 169
metal practice mute, 18
metronome, selecting, 18
Mexican Hand-Clapping Song, The, 150–153
Minuet in C, 132–135
Minuet in G, 136–140
Mississippi stop-stop rhythm exercise, 44
mixtures, 76
    exercises, 88

Monteverdi, Claudia, 163
Montichiaro, Zanetto de Michelis da, 156
mordent, 93–94
moving, fingers, 53–56
Mozart, Wolfgang Amadeus, 158, 160, 163
musical ABCs, 57
musical phrasing, 109–111
music stand, 19
music theory, 67
    key signatures, 78–83
    notes, reading, 68–78
    rhythmic specialties, 89
    time signatures, 84–89

N

names
    key signatures, 79
    notes, 68–71
natural notes, 57
natural pitch, 25
natural scale, 83
notes
    accents, 104
    bow, 2
    charts, 57
    collegno, 107
    detache, 101–102
    fifths, 61
    finger, 1
    finger-pattern slurs, 62–64
    grace, 92–93
    legato, 101
    line, 68–69
    martale, 106
    names, 68–71
    octaves, 74
    order of, 78–79
    pizzicato, 1
    reading, 68–78
    reading straight across, 61
    ricochet, 108
    scrub, 102
    space, 69–70
    spiccato, 103–104
    staccato, 103
    strings, assignment of, 72–73
    tremolo, 108
    written ornamentations, 93

O

Obligato strings, 16
octagonal shaped bows, 13
octaves, 74
    harmonics, 95–96
Ode to Joy, 123–125
one-on-one mentoring, 169
one piece back side, 12
online learning tools, 169
On Top of Old Smoky, 129–131
open elbow arm position, 40
open strings, 75
    double stops, 98–99
    left pizzicato, 96
optimization, bow placement, 34–36
order of sharps and flats, 78–79

origination of the violin, 156–158
ornamentations, 92
  mordent, 93–94
  written notes, 93

P

Pachelbet, Johann, 163
Paganini, Niccolò, 161, 164
palm line slide vibrato, 99
patterns
  A string, 72
  D string, 73
  E string, 72
  finger, 58–60
  G string, 73
  musical ABCs, 57
  slurs, 62–64
pegs
  replacing strings, 26
  tuning, 25
pencil hold, 30–31
pepperoni sounds vibrato, 100
perseverance, 31
phrasing, musical, 109–111
pinch hold, bows, 105
Pirastro strings, 16
pitch levels on tuners, 25
pizzicato, 1
  left, 96
  tuning strings, 24
placement
  bow, 103
  bow optimization, 34–36

of the bridge, 10
  finger tape, 48
playing position, 21
  bow placement, 35
positions, 21–23
  arm, bowing techniques, 39–40
  playing. See playing position
  string rolls, 37–38
practice
  bowing techniques, 29
    arm movement, 39–40
    commanding strokes, 104–106
    direction, 41
    divisions and rhythms, 43–44
    pencil hold, 30–31
    placement optimization, 34–36
    right hand finger exercises, 32–33
    short strokes, 102–104
    smooth strokes, 101–102
    sound effects, 107–108
    specialties, 101–108
    speed and pressure, 42
    string rolls, 37–38
    weight distribution of the bow, 41–43
  fingering techniques, 47
    combinations, 98–99
    fingers, moving, 53–56
    hand, setting the, 50–53
    musical ABCs, 57
    patterns, 58–60
    pattern slurs, 62–64
    reading straight across, 61
    tapes, applying, 48–49

metal practice mute, 18
notes
    accents, 104
    bow, 2
    charts, 57
    collegno, 107
    detache, 101–102
    fifths, 61
    finger, 1
    finger-pattern slurs, 62–64
    grace, 92–93
    legato, 101
    line, 68–69
    martale, 106
    names, 68–71
    octaves, 74
    order of, 78–79
    pizzicato, 1
    reading, 68–78
    reading straight across, 61
    ricochet, 108
    scrub, 102
    space, 69–70
    spiccato, 103–104
    staccato, 103
    strings, assignment of, 72–73
    tremolo, 108
    written ornamentations, 93
pencil hold, 30–31
right hand finger exercises, 32–33

songs, 113
    Ba Ba Black Sheep, 115–116
    Blue Danube Waltz, The, 147–149
    Can-Can, 141–143
    Go Tell Aunt Rhody, 121–122
    Hot Cross Buns, 2
    Lightly Row, 117–118
    Mexican Hand-Clapping Song, The, 150–153
    Minuet in C, 132–135
    Minuet in G, 136–140
    Ode to Joy, 123–125
    She'll Be Comin' Round the Mountain, 144–146
    Song of the Wind, 119–120
    On Top of Old Smoky, 129–131
    Yellow Rose of Texas, 126–128
specialties, 91
    bowing, 101–108
    fingering, 92–100
    musical phrasing, 109–111
string rolls, 37–38
tuning strings, 24
    with fine tuners and pegs, 25
    pizzicato, 24
pressed tone, 42
pressure
    bow, 42
    thumb, 52
problems, sound, 59
Prokofiev, Sergei, 165
Puccini, Giacomo, 164
Purcell, Henry, 163
purchasing *vs.* renting a violin, 15

R

Rachmaninov, Sergi, 165
Ravel, Maurice, 164
reading
  notes, 68–78
    names, 75
    straight across, 61
  sheet music, 74–75
rebec, 156
reference books, 168–169
Renaissance fiddle, 156
Renaissance period, composers of, 162
renting *vs.* purchasing a violin, 15
repeat symbols, 75
repertoire, 44
replacing strings, 26–27
resets, 105
  martale, 106
Respighi, Ottorino, 165
rest position, 21
rhythm
  bow, 43–44
  charts, 85
  exercises, 85–88
rhythmic specialties, 89
ricochet, 108
right hand finger exercises, 32–33
Rimsky-Karsakov, Nikalai, 164
ritardando, 89
rolls
  bow, 38
  strings, 37–38

Romantic era, composers of, 164
rosin, 6, 7
  bow, preparing, 14
round fingers, 51
round shaped bows, 13

S

Saint-Saens, Camille, 164
scales, playing, 80–82
Schubert, Franz, 163
Schumann, Robert, 164
scroll, 6
scrub, 102
second ending, 75
second finger, bow placement, 35
sections, bow, 43
securing finger tape, 49
selecting
  bow, 13–15
  electronic tuners, 18
  instructors, 169
  metal practice mute, 18
  metronome, 18
  music stand, 19
  shoulder rest, 17
  strings, 16–17
  violins, 9–12
setting up music stands, 19
settling strings, 20
Sforzando (sF), 111
shape of bow, selecting, 13

sharp notes, 57
    order of, 78–79
sharp pitch, 25
sharp scales, 81
sheet music, reading, 74–75
She'll Be Comin' Round the Mountain, 144–146
shift, glissando, 97
short strokes, 102–104
Shostakovich, Dmitri, 165
shoulder rest
    adjusting, 23
    attaching, 20–23
    position of, 23
    selecting, 17
Sibelius, Jean, 164
signatures
    key, 75, 78–83
        flats, finding, 79–80
        names, 79
        sharps, finding, 79
        specialties, 83
        trilling, 93
    time, 75, 84–89
signs, fingering techniques, 95
simple time, 84
sitting position, 22
sizing guide, 8
skills. *See also* exercises
    developing, 167
    online learning tools, 169
    practice. *See* practice
    solos, books for, 168
    technique books to study, 168

skips on lines, 76
slurs
    articulation, 99
    crescendo, 109–110
    decrescendo, 110
    finger pattern, 62–64
smooth strokes, 101–102
solos, 168
Song of the Wind, 119–120
songs, 113
    Ba Ba Black Sheep, 115–116
    Blue Danube Waltz, The, 147–149
    Can-Can, 141–143
    Go Tell Aunt Rhody, 121–122
    Hot Cross Buns, 2
    Lightly Row, 117–118
    Mexican Hand-Clapping Song, The, 150–153
    Minuet in C, 132–135
    Minuet in G, 136–140
    Ode to Joy, 123–125
    She'll Be Comin' Round the Mountain, 144–146
    Song of the Wind, 119–120
    titles, 75
    On Top of Old Smoky, 129–131
    Yellow Rose of Texas, 126–128
sound
    effects, 107–108
    problems, 59
    vanish, effect on quality, 9
soundpost, 10
space notes, 69–70

spacing
    fingers, 31
    finger tape, 49
special effects with dynamics, 109–111
specialties
    key signatures, 83
    rhythmic, 89
    techniques, 91
        bowing, 101–108
        fingering, 92–100
        musical phrasing, 109–111
speed, bow, 42
spiccato, 103–104
sponge, 17
    attaching, 21
square zone, 102
staccato, 103
staff, ledger lines, 70–71
Stainer, Jacob, 158
stance, 22
stepwise, 57
stinger vibrato, 111
Stradivarius, Antonio, 157
straight across, reading notes, 61
Strauss, Richard, 164
Strauss II, Johann, 164
Stravinsky, Igor, 165
strike, fingers, 54
strings, 6
    bowing the, 2
    bridge, 10–11
    change, anticipating, 56

    changing, 58
    E, selecting loop or ball, 16
    Evah Pirazzi, 16
    fine tuners, 6, 12
    metal practice mute, 18
    notes, assignment of, 72–73
    Obligato, 16
    open. *See* open strings
    Pirastro, 16
    replacing, 26–27
    rolls, 37–38
    selecting, 16–17
    sliding finger tape under, 49
    Thomastik Dominant, 15, 16
    tuning, 24
        with fine tuners and pegs, 25
        pizzicato, 24
subtracting grace note, 92
sudden bursts of tone, 111
sweet spot, bows, 42
swing, elbows, 55–56
symbols
    repeat, 75
    sheet music, 74–75

T

tail piece, 6
tapes
    applying fingering, 48–49
    sharps and flats, memorizing using, 80
Tartini, Guiseppe, 160
Tchaikovsky, Pyotr, 164

techniques
  bowing, 29
    arm movement, 39–40
    commanding strokes, 104–106
    pencil hold, 30–31
    placement optimization, 34–36
    right hand finger exercises, 32–33
    short strokes, 102–104
    smooth strokes, 101–102
    sound effects, 107–108
    string rolls, 37–38
    weight distribution of the bow, 41–43
  fingering, 47
    combinations, 98–99
    fingers, moving, 53–56
    hand, setting the, 50–53
    musical ABCs, 57
    patterns, 58–60
    pattern slurs, 62–64
    reading straight across, 61
    tapes, applying, 48–49
  practice, 114
  specialties, 91
    bowing, 101–108
    fingering, 92–100
    musical phrasing, 109–111
  tuning strings, 24
    with fine tuners and pegs, 25
    pizzicato, 24
Teleman, Georg Philipp, 163
20th century, composers of, 165

theory. *See* music theory
third finger, bow placement of, 35
Thomastik Dominant strings, 15, 16
threading strings, 26
thumb
  bow placement, 34
  hand, setting the, 50
  pressure, 52
time signatures, 75, 84–89
titles, songs, 75
tone
  age of violin, effect of, 15
  bow, effect of warping on, 13
  bow speed and pressure, 42
  sudden bursts of, 111
  varnish, selecting types of, 9
touching fingers, 94
treble clef, 75
tremolo, 108
trill, 93
triplet, 89
tuners
  auto-chromatic, 25
  electronic, 18
  fine, 6, 12
  pitch levels on, 25
tuning strings, 24
  with fine tuners and pegs, 25
  pizzicato, 24
turning the violin upside down, 21
two piece back side, 12

U

up-bow lifts, 105
upright bridge, 27

V

varnish, 9
Veracini, F., 158
Verdi, Guiseppe, 164
vibration frequency, 10
vibrato, 99–100
    stinger, 111
violin
    back side of, 12
    history of, 155–165
    holding the, 1, 20–23, 50
    origination of the, 156–158
    outfits, 6–7
    parts of, 6
    renting *vs.* purchasing, 15
    selecting, 9–12
    sizing guide, 8
    stance, 22
violinists
    composers who were, 159–161
    influence on violin design, 157
Vivaldi, Antonio, 159, 163
volume, effect of bridge placement on, 10

W

Wagner, Richard, 164
warping, bows, 13
web sites, 169
weight distribution of the bow, 41–43
Wieniawski, Henryk, 161
Wittner Taktell Piccolo metronome, 18
Wittner Traditional Pyramid metronome, 18
Wolf "Forte" Primo shoulder rest, 17
wrapped rosin, 7
wrapping strings, 26
wrists, elbow swing, 55
written note ornamentations, 93

Y

Yellow Rose of Texas, 126–128